Clif

Creating a Dynamite PowerPoint® 2000 Presentation

By Grace Jasmine

IN THIS BOOK

- Getting started with PowerPoint 2000
- Making great basic presentations
- Enhancing your presentation with exciting formatting tricks
- Learning to use the Internet to share presentations, collaborate, and more
- Reinforce what you learn with CliffsNotes Review
- Find more PowerPoint information in CliffsNotes Resource Center and online at www.cliffsnotes.com

IDG Books Worldwide, Inc.
An International Data Group Company
Foster City, CA • Chicago, IL • Indianapolis, IN • New York, NY

About the Author

Grace Jasmine is the author of more than 35 books spanning a wide variety of topics in the computer, education, and parenting areas. A two-time winner of the Parent's Choice Award, Ms. Jasmine specializes in making complicated concepts simple. Ms. Jasmine lives with her husband, Alton, and her adorable daughter Daisy — to whom this book is lovingly dedicated.

Publisher's Acknowledgments

Editorial

Project Editors: Jeanne S. Criswell, Rev Mengle
Acquisitions Editor: Steven H. Hayes
Senior Copy Editors: Suzanne Thomas, William A. Barton
Technical Editor: Jim McCarter

Production

Indexer: York Production Services, Inc.
Proofreader: York Production Services, Inc.
IDG Books Indianapolis Production Department

CliffsNotes Creating a Dynamite PowerPoint 2000 Presentation

Published by
IDG Books Worldwide, Inc.
An International Data Group Company
919 E. Hillsdale Blvd.
Suite 400
Foster City, CA 94404
www.idgbooks.com (IDG Books Worldwide Web site)
www.cliffsnotes.com (CliffsNotes Web site)

Library of Congress Catalog Card No.: 99-67521
ISBN: 0-7645-8566-5
Printed in the United States of America
10 9 8 7 6 5 4 3 2 1
1O/QZ/RS/ZZ/IN
Distributed in the United States by IDG Books Worldwide, Inc.
Distributed by CDG Books Canada Inc. for Canada; by Transworld Publishers Limited in the United Kingdom; by IDG Norge Books for Norway; by IDG Sweden Books for Sweden; by IDG Books Australia Publishing Corporation Pty. Ltd. for Australia and New Zealand; by TransQuest Publishers Pte Ltd. for Singapore, Malaysia, Thailand, Indonesia, and Hong Kong; by Gotop Information Inc. for Taiwan; by ICG Muse, Inc. for Japan; by Intersoft for South Africa; by Eyrolles for France; by International Thomson Publishing for Germany, Austria and Switzerland; by Distribuidora Cuspide for Argentina; by LR International for Brazil; by Galileo Libros for Chile; by Ediciones ZETA S.C.R. Ltda. for Peru; by WS Computer Publishing Corporation, Inc., for the Philippines; by Contemporanea de Ediciones for Venezuela; by Express Computer Distributors for the Caribbean and West Indies; by Micronesia Media Distributor, Inc. for Micronesia; by Chips Computadoras S.A. de C.V. for Mexico; by Editorial Norma de Panama S.A. for Panama; by American Bookshops for Finland.
For general information on IDG Books Worldwide's books in the U.S., please call our Consumer Customer Service department at **800-762-2974**. For reseller information, including discounts and premium sales, please call our Reseller Customer Service department at **800-434-3422**.
For information on where to purchase IDG Books Worldwide's books outside the U.S., please contact our International Sales department at 317-596-5530 or fax **317-596-5692**.
For consumer information on foreign language translations, please contact our Customer Service department at **1-800-434-3422**, fax 317-596-5692, or e-mail rights@idgbooks.com.
For information on licensing foreign or domestic rights, please phone +1-650-655-3109.
For sales inquiries and special prices for bulk quantities, please contact our Sales department at 650-655-3200 or write to the address above.
For information on using IDG Books Worldwide's books in the classroom or for ordering examination copies, please contact our Educational Sales department at **800-434-2086** or fax **317-596-5499**.
For press review copies, author interviews, or other publicity information, please contact our Public Relations department at **650-655-3000** or fax **650-655-3299**.
For authorization to photocopy items for corporate, personal, or educational use, please contact Copyright Clearance Center, 222 Rosewood Drive, Danvers, MA 01923, or fax **978-750-4470**.

Table of Contents

INTRODUCTION

PowerPoint 2000 is a comprehensive software package that enables you to create dazzling, effective presentations to deliver to colleagues at work, clients, or viewers using the Internet. Even if you've never used PowerPoint 2000, you needn't worry. Within these pages, you can find everything you need to know to create a professional PowerPoint 2000 presentation in no time.

Why Do You Need This Book?

Can you answer yes to any of the following questions?

- Do you need to learn about PowerPoint 2000 fast?
- Don't have time to read 500 pages about PowerPoint 2000?
- Do you need to present your ideas professionally in front of business colleagues or in an educational setting?
- Do you need an easy-to-use, powerful tool that enables you to get your presentation ready to go in a hurry?
- Do you need a no-nonsense approach that gets you the results you need?

If so, CliffsNotes *Creating a Dynamite PowerPoint 2000 Presentation* is for you!

How to Use This Book

You can read this book straight through or just look for the information you need. You can find information on a particular topic in a number of ways: You can search the index in the back of the book, locate your topic in the Table of Contents, or read the In This Chapter list at the beginning of each chapter. To reinforce your learning, check out the Review and the Resource Center at the back of the book. To help you find important information in the book, look for the following icons in the text:

If you see a Remember icon, make a mental note of this text — it's worth keeping in mind.

If you see a Tip icon, you know that you've run across a helpful hint, uncovered a secret, or received good advice.

The Warning icon alerts you to something that can prove dangerous, requires special caution, or should be avoided.

Don't Miss Our Web Site

Keep up with the *exciting* world of PowerPoint 2000 by visiting the CliffsNotes Web site at www.cliffsnotes.com. Here's what you'll find:

- Interactive tools that are both fun and informative.
- Links to interesting Web sites. NOT VERY
- Additional resources to help you continue your learning.

At www.cliffsnotes.com, you can even register for a new feature called *CliffsNotes Daily*, which offers you newsletters on a variety of topics, delivered right to your e-mail inbox each business day.

If you haven't yet discovered the Internet and are wondering how to get online, pick up CliffsNotes *Getting On the Internet*, new from CliffsNotes. You'll learn just what you need to make your online connection quickly and easily. See you at www.cliffsnotes.com!

CHAPTER 1

BUILDING A BASIC POWERPOINT PRESENTATION

IN THIS CHAPTER

- Planning your presentation
- Building a presentation with the AutoContent Wizard
- Entering and editing text
- Changing to the next slide
- Saving your presentation
- Previewing your presentation

In the old days, people used flip charts and felt pens as visual aids in presentations. Today, you can use PowerPoint 2000, computer software designed to help you put together your ideas in the form of a slide presentation. These *slides* are really just the pictures and words that become your presentation's visual aids, whether you show them on an overhead, on your computer, or in some other way to help make your point with polish.

In this chapter, I show you how to create a rough outline of your presentation simply by brainstorming, and then I show you how to use PowerPoint 2000 to create your first presentation. Specifically, I show you how to create a basic presentation using the AutoContent Wizard, which leads you step-by-step through the creation process.

Organizing Your Ideas

Before you even open PowerPoint, you need to organize your ideas and consider how you want to present them. So put on your thinking cap — it's time for some brainstorming. Consider the following points:

- **Ask yourself what your subject is.** In other words, figure out what you want to talk about. Consider your main idea or purpose and all your supporting points. Write them down. As you work through your supporting points, consider any potential objections to your ideas that members of your audience may have, so you can address objections before they are voiced.

- **Remember, your audience determines how you present yourself and your ideas.** As you think about what you want to say in your presentation, consider how your particular audience may interpret and react to the statements that you make. For example, if you're a doctor, you'll present your ideas far differently to a group of fellow doctors than to a group of patients or a group of HMO executives.

- **Keep in mind the outcome you hope for, to help you clarify how to present your ideas.** When you finish your presentation and walk out the door, what do you hope will happen? A raise? Funding? The renewed cooperation and team spirit of your colleagues?

Because PowerPoint 2000 relies on the structure of an outline, putting all your ideas in outline form gives you a head start on the process of using PowerPoint. The outline form that everyone learns in school — main points supported by subpoints — works just fine. So before continuing with this chapter, outline the points of your presentation.

After you create your outline, take a moment to review it. Make sure it's neat and concise. Have a friend read it to see whether it's understandable. After you feel it's clear, you're ready to put your organized ideas into a presentation that will help you meet your objectives. So open PowerPoint 2000 and create your first presentation.

Using the AutoContent Wizard to Create a Basic Outline

PowerPoint offers three options for developing a new presentation: using the AutoContent Wizard, designing a template, or selecting a blank presentation.

The *AutoContent Wizard* is an automated gallery of preformatted presentations, which are divided into categories such as "Delivering Bad News" or "Recommending a Strategy."

Templates are preformatted "looks" for slides that give a presentation a certain artistic background and layout.

Using the AutoContent Wizard allows you to create a presentation automatically — all you have to do is supply the Wizard with some basic information about your presentation and add the text you have completed in your outline. Ready to begin? Then, just follow these steps:

1. Choose Start⇨Programs⇨Microsoft PowerPoint. The PowerPoint opening dialog box appears. See Figure 1-1.

In this dialog box, you have the option to create a new presentation by choosing AutoContent Wizard, Design Template, or Blank Presentation. You can also open an existing presentation or ask PowerPoint not to show this dialog box again.

Figure 1-1: The PowerPoint opening dialog box.

Notice that the dialog box gives you the opportunity to click a radio button to disable the PowerPoint opening dialog box. Don't check this box until you are very comfortable with PowerPoint. But if you do check it and you want to create a new presentation at some point in the future, just choose File⇨New and select AutoContent Wizard (or whatever type of presentation you want) and click OK. The AutoContent Wizard will appear.

2. To select AutoContent Wizard, click the radio button (the round circle) beside it.

3. Click OK. The AutoContent Wizard - Start dialog box appears. You see a flow chart on the left side that outlines the steps you must complete in the process of using the Wizard: Start, Presentation type, Presentation style, Presentation options, and Finish.

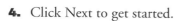

4. Click Next to get started.

As you open PowerPoint AutoContent Wizard, the Office Assistant appears for the first time. This handy feature is an animated help tool. Click the Assistant's balloon dialog box to get help with the AutoContent Wizard immediately. If you're bothered by the Office Assistant, just right-click it and click Hide. This action makes the Assistant go away until you need it again. You can call it back by clicking the question mark button on the Standard toolbar.

Notice in Figure 1-2 that the dialog box displays a list of buttons and a textbox. The buttons (All, General, Corporate, Projects, Sales/Marketing, and Carnegie Coach) represent automatic presentation choices divided by topic. When you select a specific Presentation type, the textbox to the right lists all the choices available for that presentation type.

Figure 1-2:   The AutoContent Wizard defaults to the General and Generic settings.

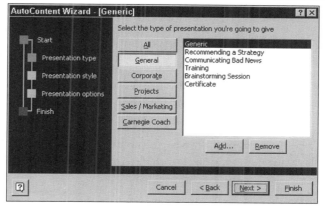

5. Consider the draft paper outline you previously created and choose the presentation type that works best for your topic. For the chapter demonstration, click the General button and then click "Recommending a Strategy." Each

AutoContent Wizard presentation type is designed to coach you through the writing phase with content ideas that appear on each slide.

6. Click Next. In the Presentation style dialog box that appears, you need to answer the question, "What kind of output will you use?" The *output* is the way you plan to display your presentation. You can select from among the following choices:

On-screen presentation: This output enables you to use your computer in front of a live audience. You use your mouse to click through the slides, which appear on your computer monitor or on a TV monitor or computer projector into which you plug your computer.

Web presentation: This output enables you to display your presentation on the World Wide Web.

Black-and-white overheads: Remember the overhead projectors that teachers use in school? This output prepares your slides to become transparencies for an overhead projector.

Color overheads: This output prepares your slides to become color transparencies for an overhead projector.

35mm slides: This output prepares your slides for use in a traditional slide projector (similar to the projector you may have used to view vacation slides once upon a time).

7. Click the radio button next to the way you plan to display your presentation. For the example in this chapter, select On-screen presentation.

8. Click Next. The Presentation options dialog box for the AutoContent Wizard appears.

9. In the Presentation title text box, enter the title of your presentation. For the example in this chapter, use **CliffsNotes PowerPoint 2000**.

10. In the Footer text box, enter your name.

11. Notice that you can check the Date Last Updated box to tell you the date you last updated your presentation, and the Slide Number Box to number your slides. Click both of these boxes.

12. Click Next, and you see the Finish dialog box. Click Finish, and the AutoContent Wizard formats your presentation for you.

Congratulations! You have set up a basic PowerPoint presentation. Each slide in this basic presentation is completely formatted with spaces for you to enter your own text. All you have to do is fill in the specifics.

Adding and Editing Text in Slide View

After the AutoContent Wizard formats your presentation, all you have to do is write your thoughts on the slides. Notice your presentation appears in the PowerPoint Tri-pane view desktop. The three panes display the Outline view, Slide view, and Notes view (see Figure 1-3).

You may notice that PowerPoint 2000 has two names for the features in the Tri-pane desktop. Slide view is also called the Slide pane, Outline view is also called Outline pane, and Notes view is also called Notes pane. The Tri-pane view itself is also called Normal view. One easy way to think of it is to use a metaphor of an actual window. If you look out a window *pane,* you see a *view.*

■ **Slide view:** Shows the actual visual aids for your presentation. This view enables you to create and edit all information and images on your slides.

■ **Outline view:** Shows the text content for your entire presentation organized in outline form. (You can learn more about Outline view in Chapter 2.)

Figure 1-3: The PowerPoint 2000 Tri-pane view desktop.

Outline view

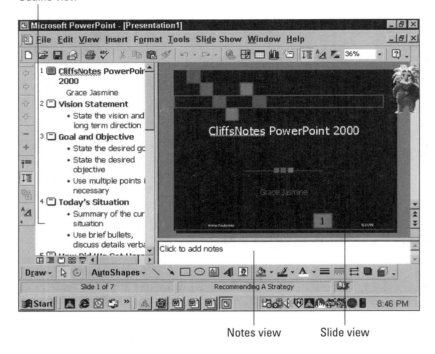

Notes view   Slide view

■ **Notes view:** Shows any notes (also referred to as speaker notes) for a particular slide and enables you to add or edit such notes at any time. Notes are the speaker's reminders about what to say about each slide and are not viewed by or distributed to the audience. (You can learn more about Notes view in Chapter 6.)

This section focuses on adding and editing text in Slide view.

Selecting a slide

To add words to a slide, you must first select the slide you want to edit. You can do so in any of the following ways:

■ Click the up or down arrows on the scroll bar at the side of your screen to move from slide to slide until the slide you want is in Slide view. The up arrow takes you toward your first slide. The down arrow takes you toward your last slide.

■ Press the up or down arrows on your keyboard to move from slide to slide until the slide you want is in Slide view.

■ In Outline view, click the slide that you want. The slide automatically appears in Slide view.

In the example presentation, you want to start by adding words to the Vision Statement slide (refer to Figure 1-3). The term "Vision Statement" is an example of a content idea provided by PowerPoint. (In this case, you can think of the Vision Statement as your main point.) Notice that content ideas appear for each bullet.

You see Vision Statement in the Outline view. Click the Vision Statement slide number (2) to move this slide into Slide view. Click the slide to edit the text in the Slide pane.

You can click and drag the pane borders to make the Slide view large enough to work in.

Adding and editing text

After the slide you want appears in Slide view, you can begin adding and editing text by following these steps:

1. Click any text. Notice that a highlighted box forms around the text that you're editing.

2. Use the Backspace and Delete keys to remove the sample text and then enter a Vision Statement. For this example, add the following text:

Create a Dynamite PowerPoint 2000 Presentation

Click the sample supporting text, delete it, and add a supporting point to your presentation. For this example, enter these words:

Learn to use the AutoContent Wizard

Your first slide, which contains the main idea of your presentation and your first supporting point, should look like the screen in Figure 1-4.

Figure 1-4: A successfully edited slide.

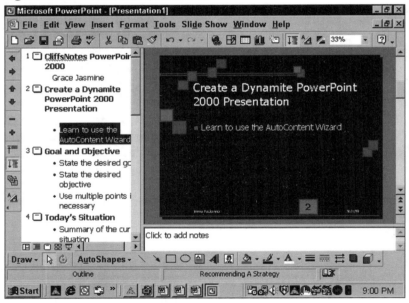

You can continue to use this procedure to complete your presentation — moving from slide to slide using any of the techniques described in the "Selecting a slide" section in this chapter and adding text from the rough outline you completed earlier in this chapter.

Saving Your Presentation

Warning

Before you spend any more time adding, removing, and editing the contents of your presentation, you want to start saving your work. Use any of these methods:

- Click the Save button on the Standard toolbar. The Save button looks like a floppy disk.

- Choose File⇨Save from the menu bar.

- Press Ctrl+S or Shift+F12.

Each of these actions produces the same result. The first time you save a presentation, the Save As dialog box appears and prompts you to name the file and select a place to save it (see Figure 1-5).

Figure 1-5: The Save As dialog box.

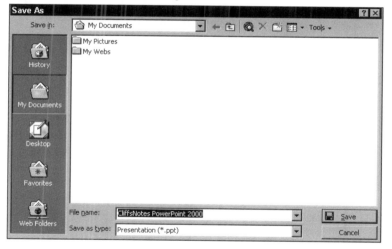

To save your presentation the first time, follow these steps:

1. Navigate to the location where you want the file to be stored on your computer using the Save In drop-down list at the top, or the file locator buttons on the left of the Save As dialog box. These buttons are located on the Places Bar.

2. Enter a name in the File Name box. Use a nice, long descriptive name. Windows 95 and later operating systems can handle very long file names with spaces and special characters. In this case, use the default name that appears when you summon the Save As dialog box. It's very descriptive.

3. Save your presentation by clicking the Save button. You've already created enough of your presentation to begin preserving your work.

Save your files often while editing.

After you save a file for the first time, choosing any of the save options mentioned earlier always saves the file in the same place with the same name, without reopening the Save As dialog box.

After modifying an existing presentation, you may want to save your changes as a new file with a different name, to preserve the original file unchanged. To do this, use the Save As function. Choose File⊅Save As from the menu bar. The Save As dialog box shown in Figure 1-5 appears again. Use a new file name to save your file.

Viewing Your Presentation

Enter all the text from your rough outline, and before you go any further, take a look at what you've accomplished. Choose View⊅Slide Show. If you're following the example, what you see should resemble Figure 1-6.

Figure 1-6: The Slide Show feature in progress.

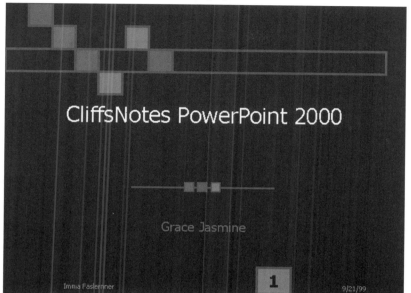

Slide Show displays your presentation in full screen. You can page through your presentation slides by pressing the down arrow key or the Page Down key on your keyboard or by clicking your left mouse button. Click the right mouse button and choose End Show to return to the Tri-pane or Normal view.

Start clicking and start talking. You have successfully created your first dynamite PowerPoint 2000 presentation.

Now that you have created a basic presentation and seen it in Slide Show view, you are ready to learn other useful features of PowerPoint 2000. In the next chapters, you learn to use the Outline view to enter presentation text and to add interesting images and even sounds to slides.

CHAPTER 2

BUILDING A BASIC PRESENTATION FROM THE OUTLINE UP

IN THIS CHAPTER

■ Creating your presentation using an existing outline

■ Inserting your outline into Outline view

■ Formatting your outline in Outline view

In this chapter, you create a PowerPoint presentation by taking an existing outline and plugging it into the Outline view. You also see how to format your outline so that your presentation clearly shows the main points and subordinating points.

In the Tri-pane view or Normal view, the Outline view pane shows your presentation in outline form.

Plugging in Your Outline

If you don't already have an outline to use, you may want to check out "Organizing Your Ideas" in Chapter 1. Once you have an outline, here's how you can plug it into PowerPoint:

1. Choose Start⇨Programs⇨Microsoft PowerPoint. In the PowerPoint dialog box, click the Blank Presentation radio button to choose it and then click OK.

If you still have PowerPoint open because of the work you did in the last chapter, that's fine. All you need to do is open a new presentation by choosing File⇨New, selecting Blank Presentation, and then clicking OK.

Either way, you see the New Slide dialog box, as shown in Figure 2-1. The New Slide dialog box lets you pick the kind of slides you want in your presentation. I tell you more about the options available in the New Slide dialog box later in this chapter, but the Title slide — the default selection — is the best one to use when outlining a presentation.

Figure 2-1:   The New Slide dialog box.

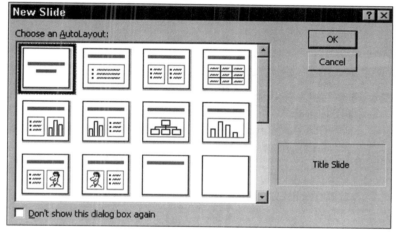

2. Click the Title Slide (if not already selected) and click OK. Your desktop should look like Figure 2-2.

3. Click the tiny slide icon at the top of the Outline pane. Notice that your cursor is in place in Outline view, ready for you to begin typing.

4. Type in your presentation title, your name and date (if you want them included), and your high-level points, hitting Enter after each. Hitting Enter adds another slide of exactly the same type. Notice that the words you type in Outline view are added to the Slide view at the same time.

Figure 2-2: With the first slide selected, you are ready to add your outline text.

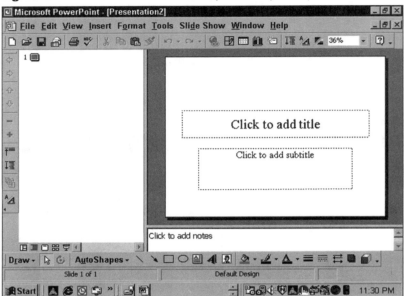

I typed "Creating a Dynamite CliffsNotes PowerPoint 2000 Presentation — the First Steps," my name, "Learning how to use the AutoContent Wizard," "Learning how to use Outline view," "Creating Dynamic Presentations – the Second Step," and "Adding Bells and Whistles" to create the screen in Figure 2-3.

You have added lots of slides, all with titles and no supporting points. But don't be concerned. I show you how to add supporting points in "Adding New Slides (And Supporting Points) to Your Outline," later in this chapter.

Figure 2-3:   Text before formatting with the Outlining toolbar.

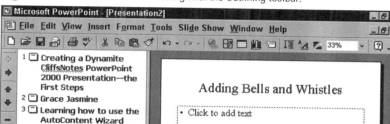

Rearranging Your Outline

In Outline view, the main points appear as headings (called high-level headings), and the supporting points (called subordinate points) are indented. Each high-level heading is the title of a slide. Both high-level headings and subordinate points are referred to as paragraphs in an outline.

PowerPoint makes rearranging headings in Outline view very easy. Just by selecting a slide and then clicking a button on the Outlining toolbar (see Figure 2-4), you can change your outline instantly.

If you can't see the Outlining toolbar — or any toolbar you need, for that matter — just choose View⇨Toolbars and then select the toolbar you're missing. The selected toolbar instantly appears on your screen.

Figure 2-4: The Outlining toolbar.

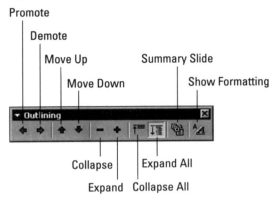

The following list explains the functions of the buttons on the Outlining toolbar:

■ **Promote:** Promotes the paragraph

■ **Demote:** Demotes the paragraph

■ **Move Up:** Moves the paragraph up

■ **Move Down:** Moves the paragraph down

■ **Collapse:** Collapses a slide

■ **Expand:** Expands a slide

■ **Collapse All:** Collapses the outline

■ **Expand All:** Expands the outline

■ **Summary Slide:** Creates a slide with the main points of all slides in an outline

■ **Show Formatting:** Shows the formatting on the corresponding slide

Working in Outline view is easier if you maximize the Outline view pane. Simply click and drag the pane border. You can also click the Outline view button, one of the View buttons directly below the Outline view pane. Click the icon that looks like an outline (if you aren't sure which button that is, hold your cursor over each View button until descriptive text appears). Outline view is instantly maximized.

Promoting and demoting paragraphs

When you demote or promote a paragraph in your outline, you are really moving the pieces of inserted text from a heading to a supporting position, or vice versa. Follow these steps to promote and demote paragraphs in Outline view:

1. Click the Normal view button in the lower-left portion of your screen, so that you can see the slides change as you format your outline in Outline view.

2. Place you cursor on a slide in the Outline pane, click to highlight the slide, and then click the appropriate Outlining toolbar button.

When you click a button, you see a corresponding change in the Outline view pane and in the slide in the Slide view pane. For example, using the text from Figure 2-3, I highlighted the slide with my name and clicked the Demote button. Figure 2-5 is the result. My name has moved up to the Title slide.

You can continue to experiment with promoting and demoting using the text from your own rough draft outline.

Figure 2-5: A completed Title slide.

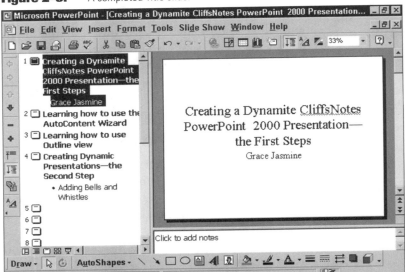

Expanding and collapsing an outline

When you expand an outline, you see all your points (high-level and supporting) in your outline; when you collapse an outline, you see only the main points, or the high-level headings. Until you have slides with supporting points, you don't need to collapse your outline, so enter some supporting points into your outline now.

Collapsing a slide can be very helpful if you want to take a look at how your main points flow, without the distraction of your subordinate points. After you collapse an outline, you can expand it again and continue to add to it. Just use the Expand and Collapse buttons on the Outlining toolbar. Refer to Figure 2-4.

Adding New Slides (And Supporting Points) to Your Outline

Once you have your high-level headings properly arranged, you can easily add new slides with supporting points. Here's how:

1. In Outline view, click the slide that you want the new slide to follow.

2. Click the New Slide icon (which has a rectangle with a starburst in the upper-left corner) to summon the New Slide dialog box and then pick the kind of slide you want. (See Figure 2-6.)

Figure 2-6:   The New Slide dialog box.

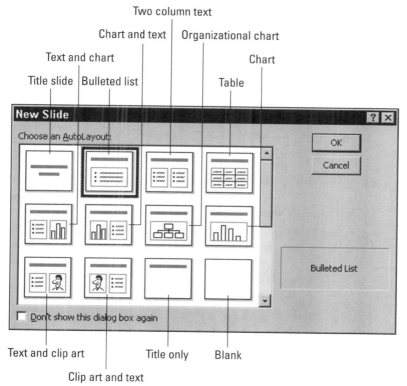

Remember

Picking the right slides as you go along is important. The following list explains each slide type in the New Slide dialog box and the slide's purpose:

- **Title slide:** Begins your presentation

- **Bulleted list:** Makes initial points, states thesis and supporting points

- **Two column text:** Compares and contrasts two things or ideas

- **Table:** Provides a table of information

- **Text and chart:** Provides information about a chart

- **Chart and text:** Provides the chart first and then the information

- **Organizational chart:** Shows organization flow

- **Chart:** Shows a full-screen chart

- **Text and clip art:** Provides text and an image

- **Clip art and text:** Provides an image and text

- **Title only:** Displays PowerPoint drawings or images imported from other applications

- **Blank:** Provides a blank slide for your own formatting

Notice that as you click different slides, the description changes in the lower-right corner of the New Slide dialog box. If you scroll down, you see a variety of other options, including slides that you can use to add media clips and other bells and whistles. I tell you more about this topic in Chapter 5. After you select a slide, notice that the cursor appears next to the new slide in the Outline view.

3. Type in your slide text but don't hit Enter (unless you want another slide of exactly the same type to follow).

4. Repeat Steps 2 and 3 as often as necessary.

Finishing Up

After you finish arranging your outline, save it as a Power-Point slide presentation. As I mention in Chapter 1, save by clicking the Save icon on the Standard toolbar or by choosing File⇨Save. Be sure to save your work often.

To view your presentation as a slide show, choose View⇨Slide Show.

CHAPTER 3

FORMATTING YOUR PRESENTATION

IN THIS CHAPTER

- Formatting text
- Using templates
- Changing color schemes
- Working with masters

After you create a presentation using the AutoContent Wizard or Outline view, you usually want to format the presentation to change its appearance. If you think of the basic presentation as your "house," formatting is the interior decoration.

With this in mind, PowerPoint 2000 enables you to decorate your presentation in a wide variety of ways. You can change the font, size, and color of text — as well as the background — all according to your personal whims. You can even use a master slide to format certain features that you want to appear in all your slides.

Formatting Text

Formatting text is really just changing the text you have to look the way you want. You can use PowerPoint 2000 to work with text in much the same way you use a good word processing program. In fact, PowerPoint and Microsoft Word share the same text formatting capabilities via the Standard and Formatting toolbars.

The Standard and Formatting toolbars

To format the text in your presentation, you need access to the buttons on the Standard and Formatting toolbars. If these toolbars do not automatically appear on-screen, you need to tell PowerPoint to display them by following these steps:

1. Choose Tools⇨Customize. The Customize dialog box appears.

2. On the Toolbars tab, click to put a check in the Standard and Formatting check boxes. (You may already see a check in the Menu and Drawing check boxes. If not, put a check in each of those as well.) PowerPoint immediately changes the toolbars that appear on-screen.

3. (Optional) Click the Options tab. If you see a check in the box labeled Standard and Formatting Toolbars Share One Row, click the check to remove it. Later on, you may prefer to have those toolbars share the same row. For the purposes of this chapter, however, you want to display the toolbars on separate rows, so you can better see the buttons available for your use.

4. Click Close.

You see four toolbars in Figure 3-1. From the top of your screen, they are the Menu toolbar, the Standard toolbar, the Formatting toolbar, and the Drawing toolbar at the bottom. You use one of the buttons on the Drawing toolbar to format text in this chapter, but see Chapter 4 for more information about the rest of the buttons on the Drawing toolbar.

The Menu toolbar is not discussed at length here, however, you'll find that all Windows applications have a Menu toolbar that you click to see the drop-down menu choices. I mention it here to help you get your bearings.

Figure 3-1:   The most common PowerPoint toolbars.

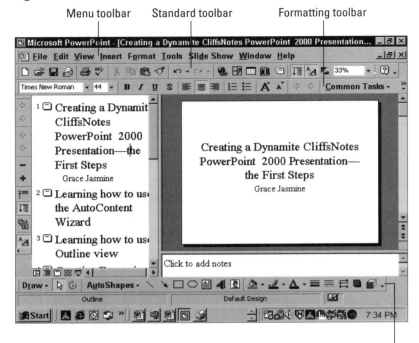

Drawing toolbar

Whenever you're in doubt as to the function of any button on a toolbar, place the mouse pointer over the button until a text description appears. This feature is called ScreenTips.

Before you begin formatting your presentation, take a brief look at the buttons you find on the Standard and Formatting toolbars. See Figures 3-2 and 3-3.

Figure 3-2:   The Standard toolbar.

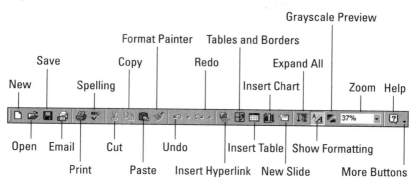

The following list describes the function of each button on the Standard toolbar:

- **New:** Opens a new presentation with the New Slide dialog box already activated

- **Open:** Summons the Open dialog box to select a saved presentation

- **Save:** Saves your presentation

- **EMail:** Mails your entire presentation as an e-mail attachment or mails a single slide in the body of an e-mail message

- **Print:** Prints your presentation

- **Spelling:** Launches the spellchecker

- **Cut:** Cuts highlighted text or images

- **Copy:** Copies highlighted text or images to the clipboard

- **Paste:** Pastes copied text or images at the cursor point

- **Format Painter:** Copies a previous text format and applies it to selected text

- **Undo:** Reverses the last action

- **Redo:** Reapplies the last action

- **Insert Hyperlink:** Inserts a URL address

- **Tables and Borders:** Summons the Tables and Borders toolbar

- **Insert Table:** Inserts a table

- **Insert Chart:** Inserts a chart

- **New Slide:** Adds a new slide to your open presentation

- **Expand All:** Expands all the paragraphs in your outline in Outline view

- **Show Formatting:** Shows text formatting in Outline view

- **Grayscale Preview:** Displays slides without color

- **Zoom:** Changes the size of a presentation in the pane that is active

- **Help:** Summons the Help feature

- **More Buttons:** Summons more buttons not shown on the Standard toolbar

Figure 3-3: The Formatting toolbar.

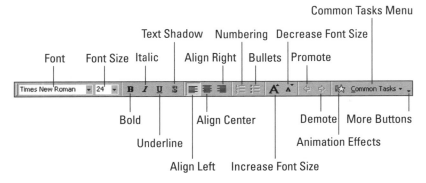

The following list describes the function of each button on the Formatting toolbar:

- **Font:** Selects font style

- **Font Size:** Selects font size

- **Bold:** Makes text bold

- **Italic:** Makes text italic

- **Underline:** Underlines text

- **Text Shadow:** Shadows text

- **Align Left:** Aligns text to left of slide

- **Align Center:** Aligns text to the center of slide

- **Align Right:** Aligns text to right of slide

- **Numbering:** Adds numbers to text points

- **Bullets:** Adds bullets to text points

- **Increase Font Size:** Makes font size bigger in incremental stages

- **Decrease Font Size:** Makes font size smaller in incremental stages

- **Promote:** Promotes a selected paragraph in Outline view

- **Demote:** Demotes a selected paragraph in Outline view

- **Animations Effects:** Summons the Animation Effects toolbar

- **Common Tasks Menu:** Summons common slide tasks to apply to new slides, slide layouts, or templates

- **More Buttons:** Summons more buttons not shown on the Formatting toolbar

Changing fonts

After you review the most common PowerPoint toolbar buttons, you're ready to format the text in your presentation. PowerPoint allows you to change font characteristics (size, color, style) to make certain text stand out according to its importance. You can use the presentation you developed in the last chapter to practice.

1. In Outline view, click the slide icon for the slide that has text you want to change to a different font. This action moves that slide into the Slide view pane. For this example, you can move the first slide of the example presentation into Slide view.

2. In the Slide view pane, click and drag the mouse pointer to highlight the text you want to change to a different font. In the sample, select *Creating a Dynamite CliffsNotes PowerPoint 2000 Presentation — the First Steps.*

3. On the Formatting toolbar, click the down arrow in the Font drop-down list box and scroll through the WYSIWYG list of fonts to choose the one you want.

WYSIWYG (pronounced, whiz-ee-wig) means "What you see is what you get." In other words, the fonts listed in the Font drop-down list box appear as they do in your presentation. For the example, select Lucida Sans. When you do, the text you highlighted instantly becomes that font.

You can change the font back by clicking the Undo button on the Standard toolbar. (You see how the Undo button can be very useful.) Change the text in the sample back to the original font.

Changing font size

In much the same way that you change font style, you can change font size. *Font size* is the size of the text as it appears in your presentation's slides. To change the font size, follow these steps:

1. In Outline view, click the slide icon for the slide that has text you want to change to a different size. This action moves that slide into the Slide view pane. If you just used the example presentation to complete the preceding set of steps, the first slide is already in Slide view.

2. In the Slide view pane, click and drag the mouse pointer to highlight the text you want to change to a different font size. Highlight your name in the Title slide of the example presentation.

3. On the Formatting toolbar, click the down arrow in the Font Size drop-down list box and choose the size you want. Select 40 in the example presentation. Notice that the font size changes on the slide.

You can change the size back by clicking the Undo button on the Standard toolbar. Return the text in the example to its original size.

If you undo a step and wish you hadn't, click the Redo button to the right of the Undo button on the Standard toolbar — the deleted step reappears.

Changing font color

Changing font color can be an interesting way to draw attention to the text in your presentation. The button to change the font color is located on the Drawing toolbar that runs across the bottom of the PowerPoint screen (see Figure 3-4).

The Font Color button looks like a capital A with a colored line below it. To change the font color of some text, follow these steps:

1. In Outline view, click the slide icon for the slide that has text you want to change to a different color. This action moves that slide into the Slide view pane. If you just used the example presentation to complete the preceding set of steps, the first slide is already in Slide view.

2. In the Slide view pane, click and drag the mouse pointer to highlight the text you want to change to a different color. If you're following the example, highlight your name in the Title slide.

3. In the Drawing toolbar, click the down arrow next to the Font Color button. A color palette appears for you to choose a color.

4. Click the color you want. The text changes to that color on the slide displayed in the Slide view pane. (Notice that the text doesn't change color in Outline view.)

   You can change the color back by clicking the Undo button on the Standard toolbar. Return the text in the example to its original color.

Figure 3-4: The Font Color button on the Drawing toolbar.

Applying Templates

Have you ever looked at the walls in your house and suddenly decided the color or the layout is all wrong and you want to change it? If so, you can appreciate the ease with which you can change the background "walls" of your presentation using the Template feature in PowerPoint 2000.

Applying a template enables you to change the "look" (the color, the layout, and so on) of your presentation slides instantly, without touching your text. PowerPoint enables you to assign or change a template anytime you're working on your presentation. To do so, just follow these steps:

1. Choose Format⇨Apply Design Template. The Apply Design Template dialog box appears, as shown in Figure 3-5.

Figure 3-5: The Apply Design Template dialog box.

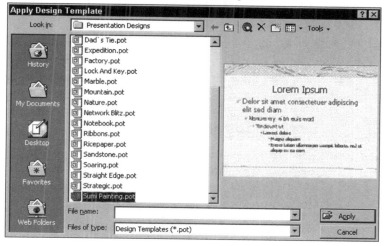

Notice the list of template files on the left side of the dialog box. Each template represents predefined formatting settings for your presentation. Take some time to scroll down the list and view the corresponding example on the right side of the dialog box. Viewing each example gives you an indication of what your presentation will look like after you apply the template.

2. Click Sumi Painting.pot and then click Apply.

You see the look of that template applied to the slide displayed in the Slide view pane. Click the Slide Sorter view button in the lower-left corner of your screen to see the Sumi Painting.pot template applied to all your slides. This view enables you to determine whether you like the look of the template or whether you need to try again. Play with this feature by selecting various templates until you are familiar with a few that you like.

Changing Color Schemes

If you like the basic "look" of your presentation but wish the colors were a bit different, you can change the presentation's color scheme. To select one of the other predesigned color schemes, just follow these steps:

1. With your presentation in Slide view, choose Format⇨ Slide Color Scheme.

The Color Scheme dialog box appears, as shown in Figure 3-6. On the Standard tab, the dialog box shows the color schemes that PowerPoint 2000 recommends for your existing presentation.

2. Click the color scheme that appeals to you.

3. Click Apply to All.

You can see the changes to your color scheme in the Slide view. The color scheme is applied to your entire presentation, including any new slides you create. Click the Slide Sorter view button to see your entire presentation and decide whether you like the new look. If you don't, just repeat the previous steps to summon the Color Scheme dialog box again and change you Color Scheme choice.

Figure 3-6:   The Color Scheme dialog box.

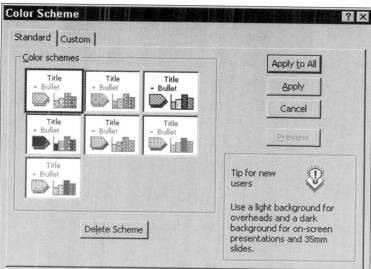

Working with Masters

While *templates* enable you to try different looks for your presentation based on predefined settings, *masters* enable you to add or edit recurring elements such as background color, objects, text appearance, and more throughout your presentation's slides or pages. Because a template holds masters, when you apply a template to an existing presentation, PowerPoint replaces the presentation's existing masters with the template's masters. To see the masters, choose View⇨Master. Each PowerPoint 2000 presentation has these four masters:

■ **Slide Master:** Enables you to format your slides and apply that look consistently throughout your presentation. Any new slides you add will also have that same look.

■ **Title Master:** Enables you to format the title slide and make it look different from the other slides in your presentation.

- **Handout Master:** Enables you to format the printed copies of your presentation.

- **Notes Master:** Enables you to format the look of your speaker notes. For more information about speaker notes, see Chapter 6.

Using the Slide Master, you can make changes to all your slides at once. Of course these changes affect text or images throughout your entire presentation. To use Slide Master, follow these steps:

1. Open a presentation and choose View➪Master➪Slide Master. Your screen resembles Figure 3-7.

2. Click the block labeled Title Area for AutoLayouts to make it active.

Figure 3-7: The Slide Master screen.

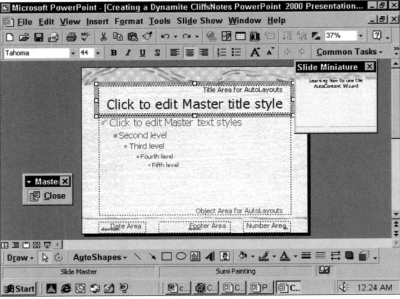

3. Click the font formatting buttons (Bold, Italic, Underline, and Shadow) on the Formatting toolbar. Notice that the title text in the Slide Master changes. Notice, too, that the Slide Miniature shows how the changes affect the look of a regular slide.

4. Click the Normal view button on the status toolbar (the lower left corner of the screen). Look at all the slides in your presentation. See how all the slide titles changed? Set everything back to normal by clicking the Undo button four times.

Across the bottom of the Slide Master screen, you see blocks reserved for the page number, date, and footer. You may be tempted to click these blocks and start typing, but there is a far better way to manage these special areas of the Slide Master.

5. Choose View⇨Header and Footer. The Header and Footer dialog box appears, as shown in Figure 3-8.

Figure 3-8: The Header and Footer dialog box.

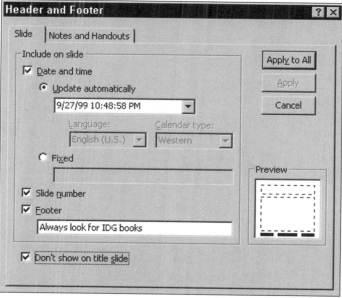

On the Slide tab, you see a pull-down menu with 13 different ways to display the date and time. You also see a check box to create automatic slide numbering and a place to enter footer text that appears on every page. In case you don't want page numbers and footers on the Title slide, PowerPoint 2000 also gives you a box to indicate that preference.

6. Choose the options you want and click Apply to All. Return to Normal view and see how your slides (but not your outline) have changed.

Formatting your presentation with the tools in this chapter is one of the ways you can give a standard presentation a very professional appearance that will impress your audience.

CHAPTER 4

ADDING ART, CHARTS, EQUATIONS, AND OTHER COOL STUFF

IN THIS CHAPTER

- ■ Adding bells and whistles to your presentation
- ■ Learning to use clip art
- ■ Being your own artist — drawing on slides
- ■ Making an impact with charts and equations

PowerPoint offers many refinements that can take your presentation from a competent one to one that truly drives your point home to your audience. A picture is really worth a thousand words, especially when you are trying to get an audience to "see" your ideas. In this chapter, you learn how to add to your presentation pictures, charts, and other cool visual aids from the Clip Gallery.

Inserting Clip Art

PowerPoint 2000 comes with thousands of pieces of clip art. These pieces of clip art are divided into categories. To find the best clip art for your presentation, follow these steps:

1. Open your presentation (if you have closed it) and click the Title slide in the Slide view pane.

2. Either choose Insert⇨Picture⇨Clip Art or click the Insert Clip Art button (looks like a drawing of a man's face) on the Drawing toolbar. The Insert ClipArt dialog box appears, as shown in Figure 4-1.

Figure 4-1: The Insert ClipArt dialog box.

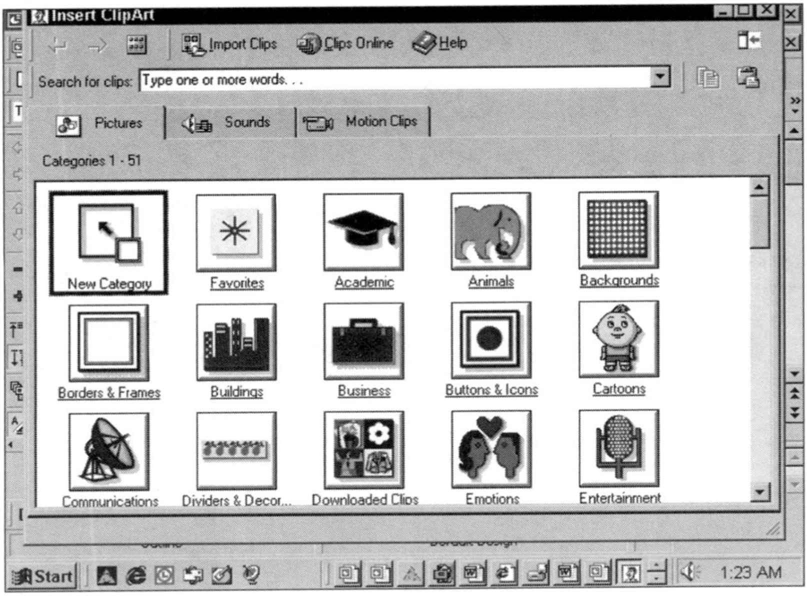

You see a variety of pictures with different category titles that are self-explanatory. Use the vertical scroll bar on the right side of the Insert ClipArt dialog box to see all the category choices. When you click a category, you see all the clip art in that category.

If you don't find what you're looking for, PowerPoint lets you search for clip art easily and accurately. To search for art, click the Pictures tab in the Insert ClipArt dialog box, type a couple of words that describe what you want in the Search for Clips text box, and then hit Enter. PowerPoint searches using the keywords you provided and displays your clip art search results.

3. Click the clip art that you want. A floating toolbar appears, presenting you with four choices:

Insert Clip. This button lets you insert the clip into your slide.

Preview Clip. This button lets you preview your clip at a size big enough to see how it will appear in your slide before you insert it.

Add Clip to Favorites or Other Category. You can use this to add a clip to the category you select. This option is an excellent way to store your favorite clips all in one place for easy access.

Find Similar Clips. When you select this option, PowerPoint searches for similar clips. Click buttons for clips with similar Artistic Style or Color and Shape, or click a keyword to search a variety of clip art choices with a similar theme.

If you're satisfied with the art you've chosen, proceed.

4. Click Insert Clip. The clip art is inserted into your slide, but the Insert ClipArt dialog box remains visible. Minimize the Insert ClipArt dialog box (by clicking the Minimize button — the one with the dash — in the upper-right corner) so you can see your presentation.

PowerPoint places the clip art in the middle of your slide. The art in Figure 4-2 was one of the offerings PowerPoint provided when I typed "award" in the Search for Clips box. Don't want the clip art in the middle of the slide? Read on.

Figure 4-2:   Your inserted clip art.

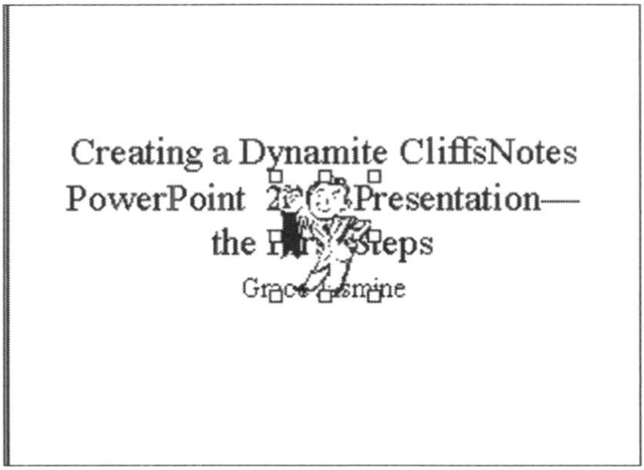

Manipulating Clip Art

After you import a piece of clip art into your slide, you need to be able to manipulate it. You can move clip art around, size it, add a shadow to it, even change its color scheme. Believe it or not, manipulating clip art is easy to do.

Moving and sizing

Here's how to move the clip art around on your slide and change its size.

1. Click the Slide view button in the lower-left corner of your desktop, so you have plenty of room to work on your clip art.

2. Click your clip art once to activate it; you see eight handles, or little boxes, around the edge that enable you to size the clip art.

3. Resize the clip art by clicking and dragging the handles.

4. Move the clip art by clicking in the middle of it and then dragging it around the screen.

If you want the clip art back to its original appearance, just right-click the clip art to bring up a floating menu and then click Show Picture Toolbar. This action brings up the Picture toolbar, as shown in Figure 4-3. Click the Reset Picture button, the last button on the Picture toolbar, and the artwork reverts to the way it was.

Figure 4-3:   The Picture toolbar.

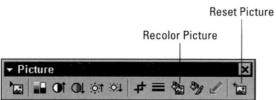

Reset Picture

Recolor Picture

The Picture toolbar (which you can close by clicking the X in the upper-right corner) contains several other handy buttons. If you hold your mouse pointer over the buttons on the Picture toolbar, the ScreenTips feature identifies the buttons. If you want to see how to use one of these buttons to change the color scheme of your clip art, read the next section.

Changing the color scheme

Here's how you can change the color scheme of your clip art:

1. If the Picture toolbar is not already showing, right-click the clip art to bring up a floating menu and then click Show Picture Toolbar.

2. Click the Recolor Picture button (the first of the two with the paint bucket) on the Picture toolbar. This brings up the Recolor Picture dialog box, in which you can change the colors in your clip art and then apply them.

The Recolor Picture dialog box has two columns of color bars next to a representation of the original clip art. The box also contains an area in the lower left where you can define whether you want to change both the fill and line colors (the Colors option) or just the fill color (the Fill option).

3. In the Original column, click the check box beside the color you want to change.

4. In the corresponding New drop-down list box, click the down arrow to display your color choices, select one, and then click OK. Notice how the color scheme changes in the clip art on the slide in your presentation.

5. Repeat Steps 3 and 4 as many times as necessary.

6. Click the X in the right-hand corner of the Picture toolbar to close it.

If you think this is fascinating, wait until you learn how to apply a shadow to your clip art.

Making a shadow

Adding a shadow really emphasizes your clip art. Follow these steps:

1. Click your clip art to activate it. When you see eight handles, you are ready to proceed.

On the Drawing toolbar across the bottom of your screen, find the Shadow button (the square with a shadow). It's the second button from the right end.

Hold your mouse over the buttons until you see the ScreenTip if you can't find the button.

2. Click the Shadow button, and a menu with a variety of shadowing choices appears, as shown in Figure 4-4.

Figure 4-4:   Shadow choices.

3. Select a shadow and watch how your clip art changes.

Now that you can size and recolor your clip art, you're ready to move on to something a little more artistic.

Be Your Own Artist

PowerPoint lets you express your own creativity by drawing on your slides. The Drawing toolbar — discussed in other chapters of this book — really becomes valuable when you are drawing on your slides (see Figure 4-5).

Figure 4-5:   The Drawing toolbar.

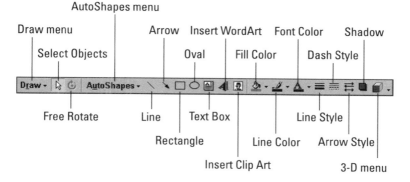

The following list describes the function of each button on the Drawing toolbar:

- **Draw menu:** Summons the Drawing commands menu

- **Select Objects:** Allows you to return to normal mouse function after using another drawing tool

- **Free Rotate:** Rotates selected objects

- **AutoShapes menu:** Summons the AutoShape menu, with a variety of pre-created shapes

- **Line:** Draws lines

- **Arrow:** Draws arrows

- **Rectangle:** Draws rectangles and squares

- **Oval:** Draws ovals and circles

- **Text Box:** Adds text in a box-shaped object

- **Insert WordArt:** Accesses WordArt to create text with interesting graphic effects

- **Insert Clip Art:** Adds clips from the Clip Gallery

- **Fill Color:** Fills solid objects with color

- **Line Color:** Changes line color

- **Font Color:** Changes font color

- **Line Style:** Changes the style of lines

- **Dash Style:** Changes the style of dashes

- **Arrow Style:** Changes the style of arrows

- **Shadow:** Adds a shadow to an object

- **3-D menu:** Creates a 3-D effect on objects

To use the Drawing toolbar, follow these steps:

1. Click the slide you want to draw on.

2. Drag the Slide view pane so you have plenty of room to work in.

3. Click the Drawing toolbar button representing what you want to draw.

4. Move to the slide, click where you want the object to begin, drag until you're satisfied, and then click. The object appears on the slide.

5. If need be, resize and move the object using the method in the "Moving and sizing" section earlier in this chapter.

If you're new to the Drawing toolbar, I recommend that you experiment with a new slide (which you can get by clicking New Slide on the Standard toolbar, selecting Blank slide, and then clicking OK). Click the Line button and then move to the slide and click and drag until you have a line. Try again with the Arrow, Rectangle, Oval, and AutoShapes. Experiment! Click Undo to erase your steps and try again.

Adding Tables

Tables are a nice way to organize or compare information in a logical way for your audience. Try as you might to stay with bulleted text, sometimes only a table will do.

Adding a table to a new slide

At the spot in your presentation where you want to add a new slide with a table, follow these simple steps:

1. Click the New Slide button on the Standard toolbar.

2. In the New Slide dialog box, select an AutoLayout that features a table. Click the examples and read the descriptions until you find one that says table.

3. Click OK.

4. In the Slide view, double-click the Table icon in the middle of the slide (this is the placeholder for the table). The Insert Table dialog box (see Figure 4-6) appears.

Figure 4-6:   The Insert Table dialog box.

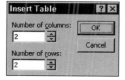

5. Enter the number of rows and columns in your table (don't forget to leave room for row and column headers!) and click OK. The Table and Borders toolbar appears.

6. Type your information into the table.

7. Format your table using the Tables and Borders toolbar. Resize the table by clicking and dragging the handles, just as you resize inserted clip art.

Adding a table to an existing slide

Sometimes you already have a slide created (because you built your presentation from an outline or the AutoContent Wizard) and want to add a table to it. Just follow these steps:

1. Make sure the existing slide to which you want to add a table is active in your Slide view.

2. Click the Common Tasks button on the Formatting toolbar. Choose Slide Layout.

3. Choose the table layout that suits your plans best and then click Apply.

4. The final steps for authoring the table in this slide are the same as for new slides. See the preceding section, beginning with Step 4.

Adding Charts

Adding charts to your presentation is just as simple as adding tables. Charts add impact to your presentation by making facts and figures easier to understand.

Adding a chart to a new slide

When you want to add a new slide with a chart, select the slide you want the new slide to follow and then follow these steps:

1. Click the New Slide button on the Standard toolbar.

2. Select an AutoLayout that features a chart. Click the examples and read the descriptions until you find one that says chart.

3. Click OK.

4. In the Slide view, double-click the chart icon in the middle of the slide. Watch as the Datasheet appears. See Figure 4-7.

Figure 4-7: The Chart Datasheet.

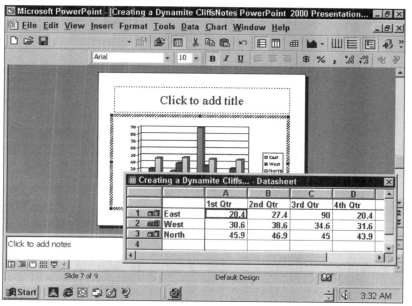

To create a chart, fill in the cells of the datasheet. Each of the boxes on the datasheet is an information cell, in which you enter the information you want to appear in your chart. When you click a cell, you can change the information inside.

5. Click a cell, enter a word or number, and then press Enter. Notice that the word or number appears in the chart on the slide behind your data sheet.

Remember to add the title to you chart slide by clicking the text that reads *Click to add title* at the top of the slide.

Adding a chart to an existing slide

Sometimes you already have a slide created (because you built your presentation from an outline or the AutoContent Wizard) and want to add a chart to it. Just follow these steps:

1. Make sure the slide you want to add a chart to is active in the Slide view.

2. Click the Common Tasks button on the Formatting toolbar. Choose Slide Layout.

3. Choose the slide layout that suits your plans best. Click Apply.

4. The final steps for authoring the chart in this slide are the same as for new slides. See "Adding a chart to a new slide," beginning with Step 4.

Adding Equations

Finally, you may want to wow your audience with some equations. Nothing convinces people like mathematical evidence. To get started in the Equation Editor, follow these brief steps:

1. Choose Insert⇨Object. The Insert Object dialog box appears.

2. Choose Microsoft Equation 3.0 and click OK. The Equation Editor window appears. (If you have not used this feature before PowerPoint can install it from your CD-ROM.)

3. Type your equation.

4. After you complete your equation, choose File⇨Exit and Return, and the equation is added to your slide.

If you want to add a mathematical symbol that doesn't already appear on your keyboard, use the buttons that appear in the top row of the Equation toolbar. To add a stacked symbol, use the buttons in the bottom row of the Equation toolbar.

If you feel you must add equations to your presentation and you're confused, begin by choosing Help⇨Equation Editor Help Topics and then choosing Creating and Changing Equations. This gets you started if you're not a math wiz but still wish to give it a try.

If you don't know the math, consider relying on mathematical "pictures" such as charts and tables to convey your meaning. If you are a mathematics buff, however, or a mathematics professor or engineer, you may enjoy Equation Editor.

CHAPTER 5

ADDING MOTION, SOUND, AND ANIMATION

IN THIS CHAPTER

- Adding motion and sound clips from the Clip Gallery
- Adding clips using Microsoft Clip Gallery Live
- Animating text
- Setting up slide transitions

PowerPoint enables you to go beyond text and pictures to adding motion and sound clips to your presentation. Although you can do much more with a professional multimedia-authoring program such as Multimedia Director, PowerPoint does come with a collection of sound and video files. If you need more to choose from, you can access the Microsoft Clip Gallery Live page on the Web or other clip art collections that you purchase in stores or download from the Internet.

In this chapter, you discover how to add motion and sound clips, as well as how to animate your text and transition your slides. By following the steps in this chapter, you can add sparkle to your presentation.

Adding Motion Clips

Motion clips are just like clip art, except that they move. (See Chapter 4 for information on clip art.) Motion clips are tiny video files, and in fact, PowerPoint 2000 refers to them as movies. But don't expect some full-length feature. Motion clips have a tiny, repetitive movement that can help you get attention when you place one on any slide in a presentation.

Adding motion and sound clips adds to the overall size of a presentation file. Don't go overboard with these effects; use them sparingly for best results.

Just as in Chapter 4 you add clip art to your presentation, here you add a motion clip from the Clip Gallery. Just follow these steps:

1. Open a presentation and, in Slide view, select the slide you want to add the motion clip to. For this example, select the Title slide of the presentation you created in Chapter 1.

2. Click the Insert Clip Art button on the Drawing toolbar and, in the Insert ClipArt dialog box that appears, click the Motion Clips tab. Or choose Insert⇨Movies and Sounds⇨Movie from Gallery. This action summons the Insert Movie dialog box with the Motion Clips tab selected.

3. To find a particular motion clip, you can type a word or words in the Search for Clips drop-down list box. Press the Enter key on your keyboard, and your search begins. The results appear in the Gallery dialog box.

If you're unsure about the sort of motion clip you want and feel like browsing, just click any of the categories displayed in the Gallery dialog box, and the choices for each appear.

4. Click any motion clip you like to select it and then click Insert Clip. Minimize the Clip Gallery to return to PowerPoint, and you see that your motion clip has been inserted.

5. Click and drag the handles to change the motion clip's size. Position the clip by clicking and dragging it to the desired location.

6. Click Slide Show on the View buttons bar to see how your Motion clip looks in action. Right-click and click End Show to return to Normal view.

A motion clip won't play in Slide or Normal view; you must be in Slide Show view to see it move. Motion clips on a slide continue to move until you go to another slide.

If you need help with inserting a clip, look once again at the information provided in Chapter 4 for clip art.

If you can't access a clip, you may have to install the clip from your PowerPoint 2000 CD-ROM. If this is the case, Power-Point asks you to insert the CD-ROM and gives you directions on how to proceed.

Adding Sound Clips

A *sound clip* is an audio snippet that you can add to your presentation. To add a sound clip to your presentation, follow these steps:

1. In Slide view, select the slide that you want to add sound to. For this example, select the Title slide. If you completed the steps in the preceding section, this slide has the motion clip.

2. Click the Insert Clip Art button on the Drawing toolbar and, in the Insert ClipArt dialog box that appears, click the Sounds tab. Or choose Insert⇨Movies and Sounds⇨Sound from Gallery. This action summons the Insert Sound dialog box with the Sounds tab selected.

3. To find a particular sound clip, you can type a word or words in the Search for Clips drop-down list box. Press the Enter key on your keyboard, and your search begins. The results appear in the Gallery dialog box.

As when you search for a motion clip, you can view the contents of any category of sound clips by just clicking the category, and the sound clips appear in the Gallery dialog box.

To sample a sound clip while still in the Clip Gallery, just click the clip to select it and then choose Play Clip on the floating toolbar.

For this example, search using the word music. (You can find many sound clips to experiment with in a hurry by searching using the word *music*.) Type the word **music** in the Search for Clips drop-down list box. Press the Enter key on your keyboard, and the results are displayed in the Gallery dialog box.

4. Click a sound clip you like to select it and then click the Insert Clip button. (Remember to preview the clip to hear it before you select it.) Minimize the Clip Gallery to return to PowerPoint. A dialog box asks whether you want the sound to play automatically in the Slide Show.

5. Click No if you want the slide to play only when you click its icon during the Slide Show. Click Yes if you want the sound to play automatically. For this example, click No. Your sound clip is inserted.

If you click Yes, your sound clip plays continuously while you're showing the slide. Just move to the next slide to make the sound stop.

6. Click and drag the handles to change the size of the sound clip, and click and drag the clip to the desired location.

Move the sound icon to a position on the slide that you like, so that it doesn't interfere with text or other clips.

7. Click the Slide Show button on the View buttons bar to see how your sound clip and motion clip look in action together. As an example, see Figure 5-1. (The slide you see in Figure 5-1 will not match the slide you have on-screen, but you get the idea.) Click the sound icon to make the sound clip begin. After you click to move to the next slide, the sound stops. Right-click your mouse and click End Show.

To move through the slides in your presentation in Slide Show view, just click the mouse.

Figure 5-1: Motion and sound clips added to the Title slide.

Adding Clips from Microsoft Clip Gallery Live

Tip

You can find motion and sound clips all over the Internet, as well as in collections you can purchase in any computer store. To select a clip from your hard drive or CD-ROM, choose Insert⇨Movies and Sounds⇨Movie from File (or Sound from File). The Insert Movie (or Insert Sound) dialog box appears. Use the drop-down list box at the top of the dialog box to browse to the location of your clip. Click OK, and your clip is inserted into your slide.

Through the PowerPoint 2000 Clip Gallery, you can connect to the Internet and take advantage of Clip Gallery Live, Microsoft's clip library on the Internet. Microsoft's Clip Gallery Live has thousands of clips available for you to use at no charge. These clips are constantly being updated, so make sure to check back often.

To use Clip Gallery Live, you must have Internet access already set up so that you can log on before you begin this activity. Even if you don't have Internet access, you can read the following steps to find out what's possible with an Internet connection:

1. Click the slide that you want to add the clip to.

   For this example, click the Title slide. Click the motion clip from the previous activity and delete it by pressing the Delete key on your keyboard.

2. Open the Clip Gallery by choosing Insert⇨Movies and Sounds⇨Movies from Gallery.

3. To open Clip Gallery Live, click the Clips Online button in the upper-middle portion of the Clip Gallery.

The first time you click this button, a dialog box appears listing the terms of acceptable use. Click Accept.

The Microsoft Clip Gallery Live Web site appears, as shown in Figure 5-2.

Figure 5-2:   Microsoft Clip Gallery Live.

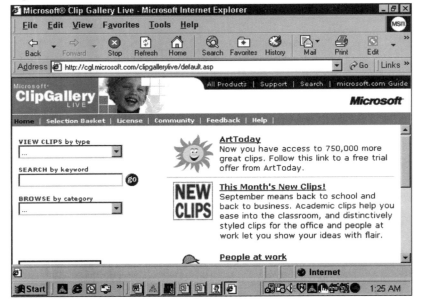

Notice that the Web site is set up to search for any of Microsoft's 750,000 clips. As you can see, this is a superb resource.

In the upper-left side of the Web page, you see several text boxes that allow you to view clips by type, search for the perfect clip by entering keywords, or browse clip categories. (Be sure to browse and sample these later.)

4. In the View Clips by Type box, click the down arrow and select the type of clip that you want.

For this example, select Motion.

5. In the Search by Keyword box, type the keyword indicating what you are looking for and then click Go.

For this example, type **speaker**.

Choose a motion clip of a man using an overhead projector.

Just as the folks at Microsoft constantly add new clips to the Clip Gallery Live, they also remove old clips. If you can't find the clip mentioned here, any motion clip will work. Remember, your screen will look different if you use a different clip.

6. Click the check box by the motion clip that you want, and you see the message <u>Download 1 Clip!</u> These words are a hyperlink, and when you click the hyperlink, the clip downloads to your computer's hard drive for you to use in your presentation. When you click <u>Download Now!</u>, the downloading process begins.

7. After the clip is downloaded, the Clip Gallery dialog box automatically opens with the clip inserted. Follow the basic instructions provided for inserting a motion clip into your presentation.

8. Save your presentation by clicking the Save icon on the Standard toolbar.

9. Click the Slide Show button on the View buttons bar to see how your downloaded motion clip looks in your presentation. Right-click and click End Show to return to Slide view.

It looks great, doesn't it?

Animating Text

Animated text is text that moves for effect. Animating the text on your slides is easy to do and makes your presentation appear more interesting and polished, making your message more effective. You can make text appear on a slide in Slide Show view using a variety of animation options. Just follow these steps:

1. With your presentation open, click the Slide Sorter view button on the View buttons bar. Doing so opens the Slide Sorter view, which enables you to see all of the slides in your presentation at once. As you can guess, the easiest way to see and set animations for text on your slides is in the Slide Sorter view.

The Slide Sorter toolbar is at the top of the Slide Sorter view. (See Figure 5-3.) This toolbar contains the Preset Animation drop-down list box. This list box contains the text animation choices for text on slides.

Tip

In AutoContent Wizard presentations, the value in this text box is often preset. However, by using the Slide Sorter toolbar, you can change effects and remove or add effects in any presentation.

Figure 5-3: The Slide Sorter toolbar.

Slide Transition Effects menu

Preset Animation menu

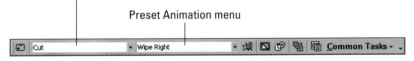

2. In Slide Sorter view, click the slide that you want to add text animation to.

For this example, select Slide Two. Notice that the Preset Animation effect for the text on the slide is No Effect.

3. For this example, choose Fly from Left. Notice how the text bullets appear to fly in from the left. Use the Animation Preview button to preview the animation effect.

4. Click each slide and set a Preset Animation effect. Sample all of these ahead of time by using the Animation Preview button again.

5. After you have selected Preset Animation for your slides, view the effect by clicking the Slide Show button on the View buttons bar.

Don't overdo this. People can become distracted with too many effects. The best idea is to set up Preset Animation and then view a Slide Show a couple of times to see if you're comfortable.

Setting Up Slide Transitions

A *slide transition* is an effect that determines how your slides appear and disappear in a presentation. You can use more than 40 special effects to move your slides into place with energy and excitement. Follow these steps to set up a slide transition:

1. Click the Slide Sorter view button on the View buttons bar. Doing so opens the Slide Sorter view, which enables you to see all the slides in your presentation at once.

The Slide Sorter toolbar is at the top of the Slide Sorter view. (Refer to Figure 5-3.) This toolbar contains the Slide Transition Effects drop-down list box.

As mentioned in the preceding section, in AutoContent Wizard presentations, the value in this text box is often preset. However, by using the Slide Sorter toolbar, you can change effects and remove or add effects in any presentation.

2. Click the slide you want to transition to and notice the Slide Transition Effects drop-down list box. For this example, click any slide. If there is no transition set, just click any of the choices in the drop-down list box.

3. Click the Animation Preview button to preview the slide transition.

4. Click each slide and select a different slide transition effect; then view the effect by clicking the Slide Show button on the View buttons bar. Right-click and click End show to return to Normal view.

Congratulations! You know how to do everything you need to create a dynamite PowerPoint presentation. In Chapter 6, you discover some important presentation packaging techniques that can help you get your presentation ready for a live audience.

CREATING AND USING SPEAKER NOTES

After you create your slides by using PowerPoint 2000, the next step is to prepare the actual speech. No matter how excellent and professional your PowerPoint slides are, you must still plan what you're going to say in front of an audience. At this stage of your preparations, speaker notes become invaluable.

Speaker notes are printed notes that you create in the Power-Point 2000 Notes pane. These notes don't appear on your slides. They're for your reference only and help keep you on track in front of your audience.

In this chapter, you discover how to enter your speaker notes in the Notes pane and then use Notes Page view to preview each page before you print it. You also find out about creating additional handouts for your audience.

Adding Speaker Notes to a Presentation

To add speaker notes to a presentation, begin by opening the presentation that you created in Chapter 1 and read through it again. As you do, think about your live presentation and the kinds of remarks you want to make about each slide.

Slides are visual aids that help support the remarks that you make in your live presentation. You, and what you say in your presentation, are still more important than your slide show. You want to make sure that you have something relevant to say about each of the bulleted points in your PowerPoint 2000 presentation.

Using the Notes pane in Tri-pane view

PowerPoint 2000's Tri-pane view is designed to make creating each portion of a presentation simple and straightforward. (See Chapter 1 for more information about the Tri-pane view.) Most people find the Notes pane the simplest of the three panes to master. To add speaker notes in the Notes pane, follow these steps:

1. Open the presentation to which you want to add speaker notes, making sure that the first slide in the presentation is visible.

2. Click and drag the Notes pane border to give yourself more room to enter your notes easily.

3. Make sure that you click the Show Formatting button on the Standard toolbar so that you can format text in your notes just as you do in any other document. That way, you can change font size or style to help you see your notes more clearly during your actual presentation and emphasize your most important points. (The Show Formatting button is easy to spot — look for the letter *A* appearing twice on a button, as A/A; that's it! If you're unsure of the name of any button, hold your mouse pointer over it and wait for the ScreenTip to appear.)

4. Click inside the Notes pane and enter your notes for each slide.

5. Move from slide to slide by using the Page Down key on your keyboard or by clicking the appropriate slide icon in Outline view. Add only the notes that you want to see for a particular slide in that slide's Notes pane. See Figure 6-1 for an example of notes in the Notes pane.

Figure 6-1:   The Notes pane with completed notes.

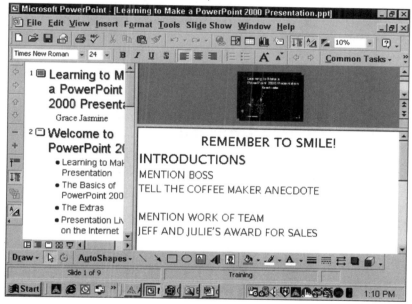

Using Notes Page view

Prior to PowerPoint 2000, using the Notes Page view was the only way to enter notes for a presentation. This process was tedious because, to see your notes clearly as you entered them, you needed to increase the zoom percentage dramatically. Although Notes Page view isn't the best vehicle for entering notes any more, it's still an easy way to see how your notes pages will appear after you print them.

After you enter your speaker notes, use Notes Page view to see your notes pages by choosing View⇨Notes Page (see Figure 6-2). Choose View⇨Zoom, select the 200% radio button from the Zoom dialog box that appears, and click OK. You can see the text you added to your notes.

Figure 6-2: Preview the look of your notes in Notes Page view.

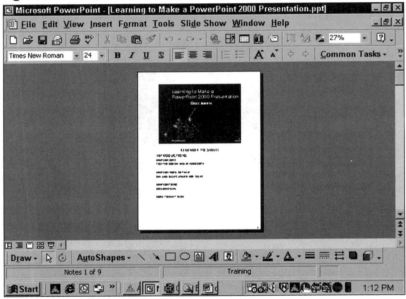

Printing Speaker Notes

After preparing your speaker notes by entering them into the Notes pane, you're ready to print them so that you can take them to your presentation. Just follow these steps:

1. Choose File⇨Print from the PowerPoint 2000 menu bar. The Print dialog box appears (see Figure 6-3).

2. From the Print What drop-down list, select Notes Pages.

3. Select the number of copies that you need in the Copies area of the dialog box and then click OK to print your notes.

Figure 6-3:   The Print dialog box enables you to print speaker notes or handouts for your presentation.

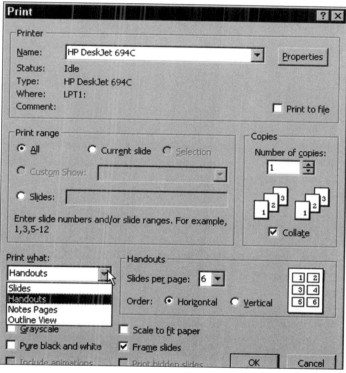

Printing Handouts

Sometimes you may find that giving your audience a handout of the slides in your presentation is useful. That way, folks can write their own notes about your presentation as they follow along. To print such handouts, follow these steps:

1. Choose File⇨Print. The Print dialog box appears.

2. From the Print What drop-down list, select Handouts.

3. Select the number of slides that you want to appear on each handout page and the order in which you want them to appear.

4. In the Copies area of the Print dialog box, select the number of copies that you need and then click OK.

In addition to printing your speaker notes for your own review and handouts for your audience, you can also print your outline. Notice the Outline View selection in the Print What list of the Print dialog box. Some speakers choose to print their outline instead of speaker notes, while others find that giving their audience an outline as a visual aid is more useful.

Using Speaker Notes Professionally

To use speaker notes in a professional manner, you must practice. Consider the following tips while practicing your presentation:

■ Never just recite the bulleted points on your slide. Give your audience members a reason to believe that they're spending their time wisely by attending your presentation.

■ Know your material well enough that you don't glue your eyes to the speaker-notes printout that you hold in your hand. Practice the material until you use your notes only for review or to keep your place.

- Practice your live presentation in front of a friendly audience of family or team members (or even alone in front of a mirror) before you present it to your actual audience. Just the practice of speaking in front of any audience greatly improves your performance.

Remember that each time you give a presentation, you become more comfortable speaking in public. Professional speakers look at each opportunity to speak before an audience not as a success or failure but as an opportunity to finely tune their speaking skills. After each presentation that you make before an audience, spend 15 minutes reviewing your performance. What aspects of the presentation went well? What can you improve? Consider each live performance a learning experience that helps you become more comfortable about your public speaking.

CHAPTER 7

HOSTING YOUR PRESENTATION IN REAL LIFE

IN THIS CHAPTER

- Using transparencies and 35mm slides
- Taking advantage of the Pack and Go Wizard
- Mouse tricks for real-life presenters

Successfully hosting your presentation requires a little planning, a few tricks, and some practice. Fortunately, Power-Point 2000 includes several useful features to help make your presentation a success. To dazzle your audience, for example, you can turn some of your PowerPoint slides into overhead transparencies — or even turn your entire presentation into a 35mm slide show. And by using the Pack and Go Wizard, you can show your presentation on any computer — even one without PowerPoint 2000. This chapter shows you how to use these handy features to the fullest effect and demonstrates a few practical mouse tricks that enable you to move through your presentation smoothly and efficiently, just like a pro.

After you learn all the features and tricks in this chapter, you're on your way to becoming an accomplished presenter in a live setting.

Transparencies and 35mm Slides

With PowerPoint 2000 available for your presentations, you may wonder why you'd want to resort to such low-tech gimmicks as overhead transparencies or 35mm slides in the first place. Believe it or not, you still find many places in the world where overhead projectors — and computers, as wonderful as they are — still crash, break, or get stolen. Many Power-Point users, therefore, keep transparencies available for both low-tech moments and emergencies. Or suppose that you need to give a presentation where no other computer is available, and you don't have a laptop handy. By converting your presentation into a 35mm slide show, you're ready to go almost anywhere! (Plus the relative novelty of "low-tech" 35mm slides and overheads in today's computer-driven society may be just the edge your presentation needs to stand head-and-shoulders above the competition.)

You get the idea — be creative! The following sections tell you how to use these PowerPoint 2000 features to do so.

Transparencies

Transparencies are those clear plastic sheets that you use on an overhead projector; you know — the kind of things you used all the time for presentations prior to computer-driven projectors becoming a common corporate purchase. If your presentation requires them, PowerPoint 2000 enables you to prepare overhead transparencies with ease.

To prepare your PowerPoint 2000 presentation for overhead projection, follow these steps:

1. Choose File⇨Page Setup from the PowerPoint 2000 menu bar. The Page Setup dialog box appears.

2. Click the down arrow next to the Slides Sized For text box and click Overhead from the drop-down list that appears.

3. In the Slides area, click the Landscape radio button.

4. Click OK.

When you're ready to print your overheads, follow the same steps for printing your presentation's individual slides that I describe in Chapter 6. Just use transparency sheets in your printer instead of paper.

Make sure that you get transparency sheets that are designed for the type of printer you're using — laser or inkjet. Otherwise, you may end up with transparencies melting inside your laser printer or ink smearing all over your presentation.

35mm slides

You can also turn your PowerPoint 2000 slide show into a *35mm slide show* that you can pop in to a carousel and mount on a slide projector.

You need to make sure that you size your slides for 35mm; then you just take your slides to a local store that can prepare them for you. (You must pay a fee for the conversion service, of course, so make sure that you research all your options to find the best deal. You can also choose to have your 35mm slides prepared by a company known as Genigraphics, which I describe later in this chapter.)

To prepare your slides for presentation in 35mm slide format, follow these steps:

1. With your presentation open on-screen, choose File⇨Page Setup from the PowerPoint 2000 menu bar. The Page Setup dialog box appears (see Figure 7-1).

2. Click the down arrow next to the Slides Sized For drop-down list box and click 35mm Slides from the list that appears.

3. In the Slides area, click the Landscape radio button and then click OK.

Figure 7-1:   The Page Setup dialog box.

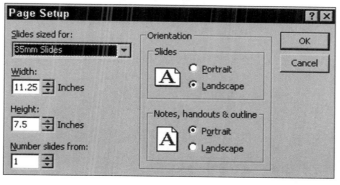

Genigraphics

Genigraphics is a company that produces visual aids — for example, 35mm slides or transparencies — from your PowerPoint 2000 presentations. You can even rent a projector from the company or have them create posters from your PowerPoint slides.

The easiest way to submit your PowerPoint 2000 slide presentation to Genigraphics is electronically, by using your modem. If you don't have a modem, however, you can save your presentation to disk and mail it to the company directly.

(Make sure that you follow the setup instructions for sizing your slides in the preceding sections, "Transparencies" and "35mm slides.")

If you're planning to submit your presentation to Genigraphics electronically, the Genigraphics Wizard that comes in PowerPoint 2000 can help you. Follow these steps to use the Wizard:

1. With your presentation open on-screen, choose File⇨Send To⇨Genigraphics from the PowerPoint 2000 menu bar. The Genigraphics Wizard appears, as shown in Figure 7-2.

The Presentation Materials radio button is the default selection. If it's not currently selected, click to select this button and continue with Step 2.

Figure 7-2:   The Genigraphics Wizard.

If you can't find the Genigraphics Wizard (or anything else that you're looking for) as you follow these steps, you may need to install the Wizard from your PowerPoint 2000 CD-ROM. If so, a dialog box appears giving you this information.

2. Click Next to move to the Genigraphics Production Selection dialog box.

Notice that, at this point, the exercise really becomes one of merely filling in the blanks.

3. Look through the various options that you can select on the remaining screens of the Wizard and click the ones that are right for your presentation. Fill in all the information that the Wizard requests, including your credit-card number, and you're ready to submit your presentation.

4. Follow the directions that the Wizard gives to submit your presentation to Genigraphics and then click Finish.

One nice feature of Genigraphics is the friendly customer-service support that you can get by calling the company's toll-free number, 800-790-4001. Sometimes, as you're making a purchase, you find the human touch helpful.

The Pack and Go Wizard

What if you're about to go on a business trip and you don't have a laptop with PowerPoint 2000 on which to display your presentation? (And creating slides or overheads isn't appropriate for the situation?) Not to worry. Microsoft thought about this situation and created a handy tool known as the *Pack and Go Wizard*. As the name implies, this Wizard enables you to "pack up" your presentation on a disk so that you can display your slide show on any computer — even one without PowerPoint 2000 — by using PowerPoint's special *PowerPoint Viewer* tool.

If you can't find the Pack and Go Wizard as you follow these steps, you may need to install it from your PowerPoint 2000 CD-ROM. If so, PowerPoint prompts you. Just have your PowerPoint CD ready.

Creating a Pack and Go presentation

To pack your presentation using the Pack and Go Wizard, follow these steps:

1. Open the presentation that you want to package and then choose File⇨Pack and Go from the PowerPoint 2000 menu bar. The Pack and Go Wizard appears, as shown in Figure 7-3.

Figure 7-3:   The Pack and Go Wizard.

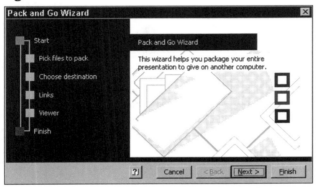

This Wizard asks you a series of questions on several screens about packaging your presentation and, in general, functions similarly to other PowerPoint Wizards.

2. Click Next to summon the selection screens.

3. Click Next after the Wizard asks you which presentation you want to include. You need to make sure that the Active Presentation check box is marked. If, for some reason, you want to include another presentation on the same disk, click the Other Presentation(s) check box and the Browse button.

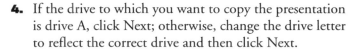

4. If the drive to which you want to copy the presentation is drive A, click Next; otherwise, change the drive letter to reflect the correct drive and then click Next.

5. Click the appropriate check boxes after the Wizard asks whether you want to include linked files and TrueType fonts, and then click Next. Selecting TrueType fonts enables your presentation to appear as you designed it, even if the fonts that you use in your presentation aren't available on the destination computer. Choose this option if you have any concern about the availability of fonts on the destination computer. (Better safe than sorry.)

6. On the next Wizard screen that appears, click the button to include the PowerPoint Viewer on the disk and then click Next.

7. After the final Wizard screen appears, insert a disk in the drive and click Finish. PowerPoint goes to work copying your presentation and the necessary supporting files to the disk. You may need more than one disk, so have a couple handy.

Click the question mark on the Pack and Go dialog box at any point to summon Help from the Office Assistant.

Presenting a packed program

The PowerPoint Viewer is an extremely simple program, which means that you can focus completely on dazzling your audience with your dynamite presentation. Here's how to use the Viewer:

1. On the hard drive of the computer from which you're going to show the presentation, create a new folder (unless you already have a folder there that you want to use). If you're creating a folder, make the name something easy to remember, such as your first name. Why? One of the first questions that the Viewer installation program asks is *where* you want to install the program. Using your name makes the destination folder easy to find.

2. Run the Pngsetup program on the first presentation disk (by double-clicking the icon) to copy the presentation from your disk to the computer. After the program asks where you want to copy the program, type the name of your destination folder and then press Enter.

Copying the presentation from your disk to the hard drive of the computer on which you intend to show the presentation is critical, because you can't run a presentation directly from a Pack and Go Wizard disk.

3. Double-click the PowerPoint Viewer icon (probably known as PPVIEW32) in the destination folder. This action starts the PowerPoint Viewer.

4. In the Microsoft PowerPoint Viewer dialog box that appears, select the program that you want to run.

5. Click Show to begin the program.

Tricks for Real-Life Presenters

Tricks are handy mouse and keyboard manipulations that enable you to move through your presentation like a pro. Table 7-1 gives you the rundown of the mouse options available to you while your presentation is running.

Table 7-1:   Mouse Command Tricks

Trick	Effect
Click	Displays next slide or build
Right-click	Opens a pop-up menu of options
Hold down both mouse buttons for two seconds	Displays the first slide

If all else fails, just keep left-clicking your mouse to move through your entire presentation.

A handy trick that you can use during your presentation is to right-click the mouse and choose Pointer Options⇨Pen from the menu. The mouse pointer changes into a pen that you can use to draw on slides. Choose Pointer Options⇨ Arrow to change the pen back -into the arrow. Table 7-2 shows the keyboard shortcuts.

The menu that pops up whenever you right-click (see Figure 7-4) contains several other handy options.

Figure 7-4:   The pop-up menu of "tricks."

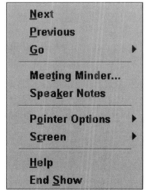

The following list describes the function of each option on the pop-up menu:

■ **Next:** Moves to the next slide

■ **Previous:** Moves to the previous slide

■ **Go:** Opens the Slide Navigator dialog box that moves you to any slide that you want

■ **Meeting Minder:** Opens the Meeting Minder, enabling you to create meeting minutes and action items as you go

■ **Speaker Notes:** Displays your speaker notes on-screen

■ **Pointer Options:** Opens a submenu that enables you to transform your pointer into a pen to draw on slides

■ **Screen:** Opens a submenu that enables you to erase pen marks or to blacken your screen (Right-click again to turn off the black screen.)

■ **Help:** Displays a variety of keystrokes to help you through your presentation

■ **End Show:** Ends your slide show

Tip

The Help feature that the table mentions is worth a half hour of your practice time. You find many interesting tricks to help you manipulate your show.

You can also control your presentation by using a number of keyboard commands in PowerPoint 2000. Table 7-2 gives you the most important of these tricks:

Table 7-2: Keyboard Tricks

Trick (Key to Press)	Effect
Enter, spacebar, Page Down, N	Moves to the next slide
Backspace, Page Up, P	Moves to the previous slide
Slide number+Enter	Moves you to any slide you want
1+Enter	Moves you to the first slide
B, period	Makes the screen go black
W, comma	Makes the screen go white
A, =	Toggles to either show or hide the pointer
E	Erases any drawing on the screen
Ctrl+P	Changes the pointer arrow to a pen
Ctrl+A	Changes the pen to an arrow
Esc, Ctrl+Break, —	Ends the presentation

CHAPTER 8

PREPARING YOUR PRESENTATION FOR THE INTERNET

IN THIS CHAPTER

- Creating hyperlinks
- Using action buttons
- Working with no-nonsense FTP site options and directions
- Using the Web toolbar

The Internet is quickly becoming one of the best ways to communicate concepts and ideas in today's high-tech society. So Microsoft is making a special effort to keep all its application software as Internet-savvy as possible. PowerPoint 2000 is no exception. PowerPoint, in fact, includes a variety of features to help you get your presentation ready for the Internet.

In this chapter, you discover how to add *hyperlinks* to your presentation that take you directly to Web documents or other documents on your computer, and you discover how to use the PowerPoint 2000 Web toolbar to view those hyperlinks, even outside a Web browser. You also find out how to add *action buttons* that enable you to navigate though your presentation and to connect to other files and Web pages just as hyperlinks do. Finally, I tell you how to post your presentation to an FTP server (or host computer) so that other people can view your presentation over the Internet or a company intranet.

Creating Hyperlinks

Hyperlinks are words or images that you click to take you to another part of a presentation — a document on your computer, for example, or a page on the World Wide Web. If you visit a Web page on the World Wide Web, you can determine whether text (usually in a different color and underlined) or even a picture is a hyperlink by holding your mouse pointer over it. If the mouse pointer turns into a finger pointer, you have a hyperlink.

PowerPoint 2000 enables you to add hyperlinks right to your presentation to make it even more versatile. You can, for example, add hyperlinks that move you to another slide within your current presentation, to another application on your computer, or to a Web site on the World Wide Web (provided, of course, you have an active Internet connection at the time that you click the hyperlink).

To add a hyperlink that connects to an existing file or Web page, follow these steps:

1. With your presentation activated in Slide view, select an image or text that you want to designate as a hyperlink.

To add a hyperlink to your slide, you must be in either Normal (or Tri-pane) view so that you can use the Slide pane or Slide view. However you get there, you need to work in an activated slide.

2. Choose Insert⇨Hyperlink from the PowerPoint 2000 Menu bar. The Insert Hyperlink dialog box appears, as shown in Figure 8-1.

Figure 8-1: The Insert Hyperlink dialog box.

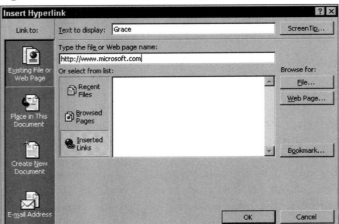

3. In the left side of the dialog box, click the icon to navigate to the location of the file to which you want to link. You have the following options:

Existing File or Web Page: This option links you to another file in another application or to an Internet Web page. If you choose this icon, you can fill in the Type the File or Web Page Name text box or select your link from these additional icons: Recent Files, Browsed Pages, or Inserted Links. You can also click the appropriate Browse For button — File, Web Page, or Bookmark — and choose a destination from the list that appears. (This feature works just as any other Open dialog box in Microsoft applications — all you're doing here is looking for and selecting your file.)

Place in This Document: This option links one part of your presentation to another part. In the Select a Place in this Document area that appears after you click the icon, choose a slide from the list as your destination.

Create New Document: This option links you to a new document that you need to create.

E-mail Address: This option links you to an e-mail address.

For the current example, click Existing File or Web Page.

4. In the Type the File or Web Page Name text box, type either the URL (the Web site address) or the file name of the hyperlink's destination. You must enter the whole path of the file or URL address — for example, **C:\My Documents\myfile.doc** or **www.microsoft.com**.

For this example, type **www.microsoft.com**, which is a Web-page URL. (*URL*, by the way, stands for *U*niform *R*esource *L*ocator.)

5. Click OK to close the dialog box and return to your presentation.

6. With your presentation in Slide Show view, position your mouse pointer over the text or image that you selected in Step 1; you see that the arrow turns into a finger. This pointer symbol indicates that the text or image is a hyperlink.

7. Click the hyperlink. You should immediately move to the document or Web site that you specified in Step 4 as the destination.

Remember

You can activate your hyperlinks only in Slide Show view.

Don't overdo the number of hyperlinks in a presentation. You need to think about the total length of your presentation and the relevancy of each link.

To remove a hyperlink, follow these steps:

1. Select the hyperlink that you want to remove.

2. Choose Insert⇨Hyperlink from the PowerPoint 2000 menu bar or click the Insert Hyperlink button in the Standard toolbar. The Edit Hyperlink dialog box appears.

3. Click the Remove Link button.

Using Action Buttons

You can also insert action buttons (see Figure 8-2) into your presentation. *Action buttons* perform certain functions that you designate at the time that you insert them into your presentation. You can insert an action button that plays a sound, for example, and another action button that moves you to a certain slide. The most common function of an action button, however, is to activate a hyperlink to move you to another part of the presentation, to another file, or even to a Web page — just as a regular hyperlink does.

Some action buttons have default functions; others do not, and you need to specify what they do in your presentation. The following list describes each action button's function:

■ **Custom:** Customizes the action that you want

■ **Home:** Displays your first presentation slide

■ **Help:** No default action, but you can define it to move to a Help feature

■ **Information:** No default action, but you can define it to move to another document

■ **Back or Previous:** Moves back to the previous slide

■ **Forward or Next:** Moves forward to the next slide

■ **Beginning:** Moves to the first slide in your presentation

- **End:** Moves to the last slide in your presentation

- **Return:** Returns to the slide you last displayed

- **Document:** Runs a program or links to a document

- **Sound:** No default action, but you can define it to move to a sound file

- **Movie:** No default action, but you can define it to move to a movie file

Figure 8-2:   The action buttons.

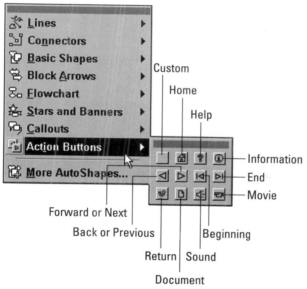

To add an action button to your presentation, you first must create the button and then define its function (or use its default setting). Just follow these steps to create and define an action button:

1. In Normal or Slide view, select the slide on which you want to place the action button.

2. Click the AutoShapes button on the Drawing toolbar and then choose Action Buttons from the drop-down menu. The Action Buttons toolbox appears (refer to Figure 8-2).

3. Click the button shape that you want to use.

4. In the slide, click at the point where you want to start drawing your button. Click where you want the upper-left corner of the button and drag the mouse to where you want the lower-right corner of the button, to size the action button the way that you want. (You size this button just as you do a piece of clip art. For more information, see Chapter 4.)

After you release the mouse button, the Action Settings dialog box appears. (See Figure 8-3.)

5. If you want to change the function of the button, use the Action Settings dialog box, as shown in Figure 8-3. Different options are available in this dialog box depending on the type of action button that you choose. (Of course, just using the button's default setting is your easiest course. The default setting for the Beginning button, for example, is Hyperlink to First Slide. If you want the slide to hyperlink to another location, use the Hyperlink To drop-down list to change the destination.)

6. Click OK to close the Action Settings dialog box. Your new action button is ready for use.

Figure 8-3: The Action Settings dialog box.

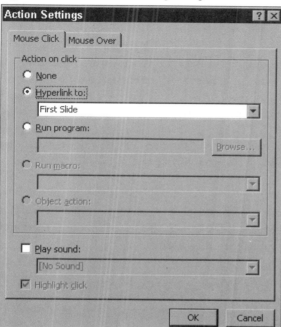

To test your action button, click the Slide Show button on the View buttons bar. Right-click and click End Show to return to Normal view.

Using FTP — Site Options and Directions

FTP stands for File Transfer Protocol. Basically, FTP is a method by which you transfer files (such as the files of your PowerPoint 2000 presentation) to the Internet or a company's intranet.

An *intranet* is an internal network of computers that many companies have — it works just like the Internet, but it includes only the company's networked computers.

Using FTP becomes important if you want to post or publish your presentation to an FTP server so that other people can view the presentation at their convenience.

In PowerPoint 2000, using FTP is really just another way of saving files. But instead of saving the files to your hard drive or a floppy disk, you save the files to an FTP server or a host computer on an intranet or the Internet.

Using FTP really involves two steps: First, you must add the FTP site address to your computer. Second, you save the file to that location.

Tip

Think of using FTP as similar to sending a letter — first you must obtain the address where the letter goes and then you can send the letter to that address.

Adding an FTP site to your computer

To add an FTP site to your computer, follow these steps:

1. Choose File⇨Open from the PowerPoint 2000 menu bar. The Open dialog box appears. (You don't even need to open your presentation for this step.)

2. Click the down arrow next to the Look In drop-down list box and select Add/Modify FTP Locations from the list. The Add/Modify FTP Locations dialog box appears, as shown in Figure 8-4.

3. In the Name of FTP Site text box, type the URL of the FTP site that you want to add. (The *URL* is the address of the site.)

An FTP address looks like this:

```
ftp://ftp.microsoft.com
```

Figure 8-4: The Add/Modify FTP Locations dialog box.

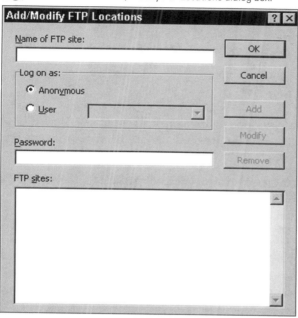

4. If the site requires a user name and password, click the User radio button and type your user name and password in the appropriate text boxes. (You must get this information from the FTP site administrator.)

Almost all FTP sites require a user name and password, and your system administrator controls this information. If this information is required and you don't have it, you won't be able to access the site.

5. Click the Add button and then click OK.

The Add/Modify FTP Locations dialog box disappears, and the Open dialog box takes its place.

6. Click Cancel.

You return to the PowerPoint screen, and your computer contains the FTP site's address.

You only need to add an FTP site address to PowerPoint 2000 once.

Saving your presentation to the FTP site

To save your presentation to the FTP site that you add in the preceding section, follow these steps:

1. With your presentation open, choose File↪Save As from the PowerPoint 2000 menu bar. The Save As dialog box appears.

2. Click the down arrow next to the Save In drop-down list box and select the FTP site where you want to save the presentation. Your computer connects to the FTP site, and the FTP site's root directory appears.

3. Select the specific directory on the FTP site where you want to save the file, enter the file name of your presentation in the File Name drop-down list box, and click Save.

Your file is saved to the FTP site.

If you're not sure about a company's FTP site address, you can contact the system administrator for that information.

Opening a presentation

To open a presentation (your own or someone else's) from an FTP site, follow these steps:

1. Choose File↪Open from the PowerPoint 2000 menu bar. The Open dialog box appears.

2. Click the down arrow next to the Look In drop-down list box and select the FTP site containing the presentation that you want to open. After a moment, you connect to the FTP site. The Open dialog box appears, listing the directories that appear at the FTP site.

3. Select the presentation that you want by double-clicking the directory icon and clicking the icon of the presentation file you want.

4. Click Open. PowerPoint 2000 downloads the presentation for you to view.

The Web Toolbar

The *Web toolbar* provides you with tools that enable you to view Web documents and documents containing hyperlinks while you're still in PowerPoint 2000. The toolbar contains some of the same ease-of-navigation functions that you find in any Web browser with which you're familiar.

To access the Web toolbar shown in Figure 8-5, choose View⇨Toolbars⇨Web from the PowerPoint 2000 menu bar.

Figure 8-5:   The Web toolbar.

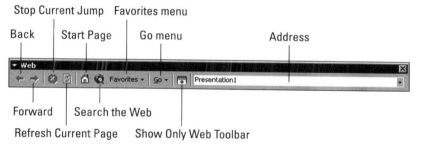

Stop Current Jump   Favorites menu

Back   Start Page   Go menu   Address

Forward   Search the Web

Refresh Current Page   Show Only Web Toolbar

The following bullet list describes the function of each Web toolbar button:

■ **Back:** Moves backward to the previous slide or page

■ **Forward:** Moves forward to the next slide or page

■ **Stop Current Jump:** Stops the page you're connecting to from loading

■ **Refresh Current Page:** Reloads the current page

- **Start Page:** Moves to the start page

- **Search the Web:** Opens your default browser's search engine

- **Favorites menu:** Displays your favorites list

- **Go menu:** Enables you to access a variety of functions from a drop-down menu, including opening a file, going backward or forward, moving to your home page, and searching the Web by opening your default browser

- **Show Only Web Toolbar:** Hides all the other toolbars, leaving only the Web toolbar on-screen

- **Address:** Text box that displays the current slide's address or Web page's URL; you can also use this text box to navigate to any address

The tools that you learn to use in this chapter enable you to share PowerPoint 2000 presentations globally by using the Internet. In Chapter 9, you learn even more ways to make the Internet work for you as a PowerPoint presenter.

HOSTING YOUR PRESENTATION ON THE INTERNET

IN THIS CHAPTER

- Putting a presentation on the Web
- Setting up a NetMeeting
- Broadcasting a presentation
- Using Web Discussions and E-mail Subscriptions features

PowerPoint 2000 enables you to host a presentation not only in the physical world (such as a meeting room), but in the "virtual" world as well, such as on the Internet or a company intranet. Just imagine: While you're asleep or on vacation, your presentation can be impressing potential clients or co-workers — and they never have to leave their desks. Power-Point also lets you collaborate with others to create a presentation and keeps you up to date on the changes the rest of the team is making. This chapter shows you how to take advantage of these features.

Publishing a Presentation on the Web

You can actually convert your presentation to HTML format and publish your presentation on the Web. That way, anyone with Internet access can view your presentation online using his or her own browser.

HTML stands for *Hyper Text Markup Language* and is a Web page programming language. If you convert your presentation to HTML format, you're really just saving your presentation as a Web page.

As you can imagine, HTML is a very important tool for you as a PowerPoint user. But don't worry — you really don't need to know a thing about HTML or even much about the Internet to publish your presentation on the Web. You just need to know how to save your presentation as a Web page, and then you need a Web server to post it to.

Saving your presentation as a Web page

Follow these steps to save your presentation as a Web page:

1. Choose File⇨Save as Web Page from the PowerPoint 2000 menu bar. The Save As dialog box appears.

   If your File menu doesn't show the Save as Web Page option, hold your pointer over the downward arrows at the bottom of the menu. That produces an expanded File menu with the Save as Web Page option.

2. Click Publish.

   The Publish as Web Page dialog box appears, which enables you to customize your Web page using the following options:

   Publish What?: Specify whether you're publishing the entire presentation or just a few slides. You can choose to display speaker notes, too.

   You can even click Web Options to further customize your presentation in the Web Options dialog box, which has four tabs: General, Files, Pictures, and Encoding. On the General tab, you can make selections about your presentation's appearance; on the Files tab, you can choose file-naming and locating options for the Web files; on the Pictures tab, you can choose picture file formats; and on the Encoding tab, you can choose among browser-language options.

Browser Support: Choose which browser your presentation will appear on.

Most of the time, you can't be sure what type of browser your audience is going to use to view your presentation online. Choose the third option, *All Browsers Listed Above*, to make sure that your presentation supports all browser choices.

Publish a Copy As: You can change the name of your presentation, or you can change the location where you want the files stored.

Open Published Web Page in Browser: You can view your presentation as a Web page after you save it as one.

3. After you make your selections in the Publish as Web Page dialog box, click Publish to save your presentation.

The presentation automatically becomes an HTML document, and the filename has an HTM extension.

Publishing your Web page to the World Wide Web

To publish anything to the World Wide Web, you must have space on a Web server that you're authorized to use. If you're publishing for your company, ask the system administrator about company procedures for saving Web pages to the server. If you're publishing the presentation yourself, ask your Internet Service Provider (ISP) about available space and the rules for its use. Many ISPs provide free Web space.

Follow these steps to publish to the Web:

1. In PowerPoint, open the presentation you saved in HTML.

2. Choose File⇨Save as Web Page and then click Publish to open the Publish as Web Page dialog box.

3. In the File Name text box, type the URL (address) of the server to which you want to save your files.

4. Click Save. PowerPoint connects to the Web server, and you can see the folders saved to the site.

5. Hold your mouse pointer over the File Name text box. Your file's name appears.

6. Click Save. PowerPoint saves your presentation to the Web.

After you save your presentation to the Web, you can view it by using your browser. Just choose File⇨Web Page Preview.

Scheduling a NetMeeting

If you ever collaborate with colleagues on PowerPoint 2000 documents, NetMeeting is a tool you're likely to use a lot. By using NetMeeting, you can chat, draw pictures, and even talk (if you have microphones) over the Internet, thereby increasing your efficiency without ever leaving PowerPoint.

Before you use NetMeeting, make sure that you and the other meeting participants agree on a time and a server on which to hold your meeting. Determine the host of the meeting so that everyone knows whose name to look for online. Ask your system administrator to set up the meeting so that only those who know a certain password can attend.

If you're using a company intranet, you're more than likely assigned a server; otherwise, Microsoft makes a few Internet servers available to the public. You're free to use any of these servers that you want.

To use NetMeeting, follow these steps:

1. In PowerPoint, choose Tools⇨Online Collaboration⇨ Meet Now. The Place a Call dialog box appears.

2. At the Directory text box, select the chosen server from the drop-down list or type the server's address yourself.

3. If you're the designated host, press Cancel to go back to PowerPoint 2000 and wait for the rest of the audience to find you.

   If you're a participant, click the host's name on the list of people connected to the meeting server.

NetMeeting launches, and if this is the first time you've run NetMeeting, it prompts you to fill in some information. After you finish, you find yourself back in PowerPoint. Notice that PowerPoint adds the Online Meeting toolbar to your screen.

If you're in control of the meeting, other participants can just sit back, watch the show, and discuss the presentation materials with you. Even if you switch to Slide Show mode, your Online Meeting toolbar stays on-screen for you to use as you need it (see Figure 9-1).

The following list describes the function of each button on the Online Meeting toolbar:

▪ **Participant List:** Lists all your meeting members

▪ **Call Participant:** Adds members to your meeting

▪ **Remove Participant:** Excuses participants from the meeting

- ■ **Allow Others to Edit:** Switches control of the application to another meeting member

- ■ **Display Chat Window:** Opens another window for a chat-room style dialog between meeting members

- ■ **Display Whiteboard:** Opens up another window for freehand and special shape illustrations

- ■ **End Meeting:** Hangs up the call

Figure 9-1: The Online Meeting toolbar.

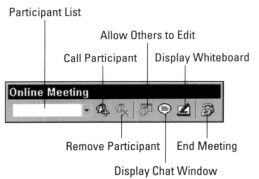

Participant List

Allow Others to Edit

Call Participant   Display Whiteboard

Online Meeting

Remove Participant   End Meeting

Display Chat Window

Using the Presentation Broadcast Feature

What would you do if you had a presentation scheduled but couldn't travel to that location? In the old days, you'd have needed to reschedule your presentation, possibly leaving your audience angry and frustrated. But by using the PowerPoint 2000 Presentation Broadcast feature, you can give your presentation without ever leaving your office.

One nice aspect of this feature is that your audience members don't need PowerPoint 2000 to view your broadcast. They only need their Internet connection and browser, which makes this feature a wonderful tool for selling a product or showing a broadcast to potential clients.

The first time that you use the Presentation Broadcast feature, you may need to install it from your PowerPoint CD-ROM.

To use Presentation Broadcast, you need to set up your computer to share files with the appropriate people, and then you need to schedule the broadcast.

Setting up your computer to share files

Follow these steps to set up your computer to share files:

1. Double-click My Computer on the desktop and then open your Control Panel.

2. Double-click Network. The Network dialog box opens.

3. On the Configuration tab, click the File and Print Sharing button. The File and Print Sharing dialog box appears.

4. Make sure that the check box for sharing files is marked. Click OK, and you return to the Configuration tab on the Network dialog box.

5. Before leaving the Network dialog box, click the Identification tab and copy down the information in the Computer Name box. This name is the name of your computer, and later you must use it to direct others to your presentation. Click OK after you finish.

6. After you change the File and Print Sharing setting, reboot your computer for the change to take effect.

7. In Windows Explorer, highlight the folder you want to share by clicking it.

8. Choose File⇨Properties from the Explorer menu bar.

9. Click the Sharing tab in the dialog box that appears. Click the Shared As radio button to select it, and notice the exact Share Name of that folder.

Scheduling the broadcast

After you set up your folder for sharing, you need to schedule the broadcast:

1. In PowerPoint 2000, choose Slide Show⇨Online Broadcast⇨Set Up and Schedule from the menu bar. The Broadcast Schedule dialog box appears.

PowerPoint may tell you that the Online Broadcast feature wasn't included in your installation. If so, just have the PowerPoint CD ready.

2. Click the Set Up and Schedule a New Broadcast radio button to select it and then click OK.

3. In the Schedule a New Broadcast dialog box, fill in all the information on the Description tab. This information appears on your Lobby Page, which offers preview information about your broadcast to your meeting viewers. You can preview the Lobby Page in your Internet browser by clicking Preview Lobby Page. An example of a Lobby Page is shown in Figure 9-2.

The Schedule a New Broadcast dialog box doesn't include a spell-check function. Carefully review the information before saving your message. Just as in a regular presentation, typos and other errors are especially embarrassing if you display them to an audience.

4. On the Broadcast Settings tab, fill in the necessary information and click Server Options.

Figure 9-2:   The Presentation Broadcast Lobby Page.

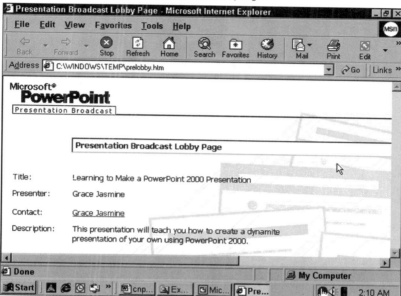

5. In the Server Options dialog box (see Figure 9-3), enter the name of your computer and the drive that you set up for sharing. You must enter the name in the following format: **\\computername\foldername** (where *computername* is the name in the Computer Name box from Step 5 in the preceding section, "Setting up your computer to share files," and *foldername* is the shared folder name from Step 9 in that same section).

6. Click OK to return to the Schedule a New Broadcast dialog box and click the Schedule Broadcast button.

The Microsoft Outlook Meeting Schedule and Invitation dialog box appears. Make sure that you have the time correct. You can use Outlook to mail invitations to planned attendees. After you send and save this appointment, PowerPoint 2000 gives you a message confirming your schedule.

Figure 9-3: The Server Options dialog box.

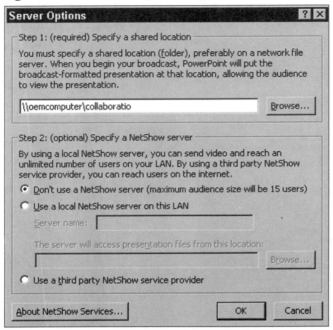

7. Click OK.

8. At the appointed time, open your presentation in PowerPoint and choose Slide Show⇨Online Broadcast⇨ Begin Broadcast from the menu bar.

9. Click Start, and you go live and on the air with your meeting attendees.

Your meeting attendees may use their own Web browsers to view this presentation; they don't need PowerPoint 2000 software installed.

Web Discussions and E-mail Subscriptions

Web Discussions and E-mail Subscriptions are two other tools to use among team members. Everyone who participates needs PowerPoint 2000 software.

You use Web Discussions for discussing a presentation, and you use E-mail Subscriptions to notify others via e-mail of changes that you make to a presentation.

Web Discussions

To use the Web Discussions feature, your Web server must have Office Server Extensions on it. Ask your system administrator whether your server has the correct extensions and, if it does, ask for the correct server address.

Follow these steps to be collaborating in minutes:

1. In PowerPoint 2000, choose Tools⇨Online Collaboration⇨Web Discussions from the menu bar.

2. In the text box of the Add or Edit Discussion Servers dialog box, type the server name you got from your system administrator.

3. Click OK. The Discussion Options dialog box appears (see Figure 9-4).

In this dialog box, you can choose different fields to display, such as the time or subject.

Figure 9-4: The Discussion Options dialog box.

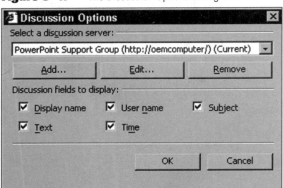

4. Select the options that you want. You may need to use this service a few times before you figure out what works best for you.

5. Click OK.

PowerPoint displays the Web Discussion toolbar and the discussion pane. The discussion pane is like a built-in chat room that enables participants to see each other's comments.

6. Click the Insert Discussion button on the Web Discussion toolbar to join in the conversation.

The Web Discussions feature is best for posting on the Internet or company intranet and giving team members a few days to review and comment.

Subscribing to changes by e-mail

Sometimes, as a team of people work simultaneously on a document, monitoring the changes can prove annoying. PowerPoint 2000 enables you to subscribe to an e-mail distribution list that sends out notices whenever someone makes changes to a specific file or folder. This feature is known as E-mail Subscriptions. To use it, follow these steps:

1. Click the Document Subscription button on the Web Discussion toolbar.

You see a Document Subscription dialog box asking you to fill out information regarding which file you want to follow up on, under what conditions you want to be notified, how you can be reached by e-mail, and how often you need these updates.

2. Click OK and watch the mail. Keeping up with changes is very easy this way.

There, you have all the nuts and bolts of creating a dynamite PowerPoint presentation — one that you can present before a live audience and one that you can deliver over the Internet. After reading this CliffsNotes book, you understand how to use a tool that can prove instrumental in helping you achieve your professional goals.

CLIFFSNOTES REVIEW

Use this CliffsNotes Review to practice what you've learned in this book and to build your confidence in doing the job right the first time. After you work through the review questions, the problem-solving exercises, the visual test, and the fun and useful practice project, you're well on your way to achieving your goal of creating dynamite PowerPoint presentations every time you try.

Q&A

1. An outline is an important preparation step in creating a PowerPoint presentation because

   a. An outline helps you clarify your thoughts.

   b. An outline helps you organize your ideas.

   c. An outline helps you enter information into Outline view.

   d. All of the above.

2. The AutoContent Wizard is helpful for first time PowerPoint users because

   a. It writes your presentation for you.

   b. It leads you through preformatted presentation types that are useful for a variety of different presentations.

   c. First-time users are never able to master creating a new presentation from blank slides.

3. The PowerPoint Tri-pane desktop consists of

   a. Outline view, Slide Sorter View, and Notes Page view.

   b. Outline view, Slide Show view, and Presentation view.

   c. Outline pane, Slide pane, and Notes pane.

4. To add text to an AutoContent Wizard slide, you

   a. Click the slide and enter text where the cursor activates, deleting example text as you go.

   b. Add text in Outline view, deleting example text as you go.

   c. Add text in the Notes pane and click Save As.

   d. Both a and b.

5. Slide Sorter view allows you to

   a. Sort your slides in alphabetical order.

   b. See the slides saved as Web pages.

   c. See all of the slides in your presentation at once, reduced in size.

6. To add clip art to a presentation you

   a. Click the Drawing toolbar button called Insert Clip Art.

   b. Click the New Slide icon on the Standard toolbar.

   c. Choose Insert⇨Picture⇨Clip Art.

   d. Both a and c.

7. You can find helpful hints about presenting a slide show by

   a. Clicking on the Slide Show button.

   b. Left-clicking your mouse and clicking Help as you present a slide show.

   c. Right-clicking you mouse and clicking Help as you present a slide show.

8. PowerPoint 2000 allows you to

   a. Save your presentations in HTML format.

   b. Save your presentations to FTP sites.

   c. Save your presentations as Web pages.

   d. All of the above.

9. The most important part of your PowerPoint presentation is

a. Your speaker notes.

b. Your handouts.

c. You and your message about your topic.

Answers: (1) d. (2) b. (3) c. (4) d. (5) c. (6) d. (7) c. (8) d. (9) c.

Scenarios

1. You are traveling to another city to give your presentation at a vendor's firm. You have never been there before and aren't sure about the setup for your live presentation. You should

_____

_____

2. You are trying to save your presentation to the company's FTP site and aren't having any success. You should

_____

_____

Answers: (1) Use the Pack and Go Wizard to save your presentation file with the PowerPoint Viewer and consider taking overhead transparency copies of your slides. (2) Contact your company's system administrator to make sure you have the necessary password information.

Visual Test

Name the View buttons shown here.

Figure R-1:   The View buttons.

Answers: Tri-pane or Normal view, Outline view, Slide view, Slide Sorter view, Slide Show view

Consider This

- Did you know that you can copy the PowerPoint Viewer as many times as you want and distribute it freely to anyone who wants to view your presentation?

- Did you know that you can send your PowerPoint presentation as an e-mail attachment to the person you are going to present it to, letting that person view it ahead of time in preparation for your live meeting?

Practice Project

1. Use the AutoContent Wizard to set up several different kinds of practice presentations. Go through each step of creating a presentation and then, using the Slide Show feature of PowerPoint, talk through your presentation aloud. Practice presenting a topic without making speaker notes to become comfortable in front of an audience.

2. Create your presentation and practice it several different ways:

- Using overhead transparencies and an overhead projector
- Using your computer and driving your presentation with the mouse
- As a presentation broadcast
- As a Web discussion

3. Use a microphone and your sound recorder (in Windows 95 or greater) to make a sound file of your own voice as an introduction to your PowerPoint presentation. Then, use the Clip Gallery to insert your sound file into your presentation.

4. Get together with team members for a presentation night. Give everyone a chance to practice his or her presentation in front of a friendly audience and give each member of the team constructive feedback. Consider using a video camera to capture presentations so that each member of the team can view himself or herself in action.

CLIFFSNOTES RESOURCE CENTER

The learning doesn't need to stop here. CliffsNotes Resource Center shows you the best of the best — links to the best information in print and online about PowerPoint 2000. Look for all the terrific resources at your favorite bookstore or local library and on the Internet. When you're online, make your first stop www.cliffsnotes.com, where you'll find more incredibly useful information about PowerPoint 2000.

Books

This CliffsNotes book is one of many great books about PowerPoint 2000 published by IDG Books Worldwide, Inc., and other publishers. So if you want some great next-step books, check out these other publications:

PowerPoint 2000 For Windows For Dummies, by Doug Lowe with Grace Jasmine, gives you an in-depth look at PowerPoint 2000 with lots of insight about how the application has been modified since PowerPoint 97. IDG Books Worldwide, Inc. $19.95.

Microsoft Office 2000 9 in 1 For Dummies Desk Reference, by multiple authors, is nine books in one, giving an interesting once-over for all the Office 2000 applications: Windows 98, Word, Excel, Access, Outlook, PowerPoint, FrontPage, Publisher, and PhotoDraw. IDG Books Worldwide, Inc. $29.99.

Microsoft Pocket Guide to PowerPoint 2000, by Stephen L. Nelson, gives you a look at PowerPoint 2000 from the company that developed it. Microsoft Corporation. $12.99.

Mastering the Art of Public Speaking, by Peter Desberg, helps you develop the skills necessary to master speaking before an audience. Barnes and Noble Books. $6.98.

You can easily find books published by IDG Books Worldwide, Inc., and other publishers in your favorite bookstores, at the library, on the Internet, and at a store near you. We also have three Web sites that you can use to read about all the books we publish:

- www.cliffsnotes.com
- www.dummies.com
- www.idgbooks.com

Internet

Check out these Web sites for information about PowerPoint 2000:

Microsoft Product and Technology Catalog, http:// microsoft.com/catalog/, gives you the latest and greatest information about PowerPoint and the other Office 2000 applications.

Beyond.com Microsoft Showcase, http://www. beyond.com/showcase/microsoft.htm, is a great site if you're interested in buying some more Microsoft software. Next time you're on the Internet, check it out.

Toastmasters International, http://www.toastmasters.org/, is the Web site for the most widely recognized public speaking organization in the world. An important aspect of presenting a PowerPoint presentation is fine-tuning your speaking skills, and this site offers speaking tips, the locations of local groups, and a host of other useful information.

Next time you're on the Internet, don't forget to drop by www.cliffsnotes.com. We created an online Resource Center that you can use, today, tomorrow, and beyond.

Send Us Your Favorite Tips

In your quest for learning, have you ever experienced that sublime moment when you figure out a trick that saves time or trouble? Perhaps you realized you were taking ten steps to accomplish something that could take two. Or you found a little-known workaround that achieved great results. If you've discovered a useful tip that helped you use PowerPoint 2000 more effectively and you'd like to share it, the CliffsNotes staff would love to hear from you. Go to our Web site at www.cliffsnotes.com and click the Talk to Us button. If we select your tip, we may publish it as part of *CliffsNotes Daily*, our exciting, free e-mail newsletter. To find out more or to subscribe to a newsletter, go to www.cliffsnotes.com on the Web.

INDEX

A

action buttons, 84, 88-89, 91
animated text, 62–63. *See also* motion clips
Apply Design Template dialog box, 35
audio. *See* sound clips
AutoContent Wizard, 5–9, 12, 62

B

books, recommended, 2, 115–116

C

charts, 24, 30, 50, 52
CliffsNotes Daily, 2, 117
clip art, 24, 41–42, 44–47
color
font, 34
schemes, 36, 45
Color Scheme dialog box, 36

D

dates, last updated, 9
Drawing toolbar, 27, 41, 46–49

E

editing text, 11, 12. *See also* formatting
E–mail Subscriptions, 107–108
equations, 52–53

F

file sharing, 103
File Transfer Protocol (FTP). *See* FTP (File Transfer Protocol)
filenames, 14
fonts, 31–34, 79
formatting. *See also* editing text
text, 26–28, 30, 32–34
toolbars, 27–29, 31
using fonts, 32–33
Formatting toolbar, 27–28, 31, 33
FTP (File Transfer Protocol), 91–92, 94–95

G

Genigraphics, 75–77

H

handout copies, of slides, 69–70
headers and footers, 39–40
Help feature, 7, 30, 82
HTML (HyperText Markup Language), 98
hyperlinks, 30, 84–87

I

icons, used in this book, 2
ideas, organizing your, 4–5
Insert ClipArt dialog box, 41–42
Internet. *See* FTP (File Transfer Protocol); Web presentations; Web sites
intranets, 84, 91, 101

CliffsNotes™

Your shortcut to
success™
for over 40 years

Computers and Software
Confused by computers? Struggling with software? Let
CliffsNotes get you up to speed on the fundamentals —
quickly and easily. Titles include:

Balancing Your Checkbook with Quicken®
Buying Your First PC
Creating a Dynamite PowerPoint® 2000 Presentation
Making Windows® 98 Work for You
Setting up a Windows® 98 Home Network
Upgrading and Repairing Your PC
Using Your First PC
Using Your First iMac™
Writing Your First Computer Program

The Internet
Intrigued by the Internet? Puzzled about life online?
Let *CliffsNotes* show you how to get started with e–mail,
Web surfing, and more. Titles include:

Buying and Selling on eBay®
Creating Web Pages with HTML
Creating Your First Web Page
Exploring the Internet with Yahoo!®
Finding a Job on the Web
Getting on the Internet
Going Online with AOL®
Shopping Online Safely